W9-BUG-453

365 days of Creative play

For Children 2 years and up

4th Edition

Sheila Ellison and Dr. Judith Gray

SOURCEBOOKS, INC.®
NAPERVILLE, ILLINOIS

Copyright © 2005, 1995 by Sheila Ellison and Dr. Judith Gray
Cover and internal design © 2005, 1995 by Sourcebooks, Inc.
Cover photos © Photodisc, Digital Vision, Rubberball Productions, Comstock
Sourcebooks and the colophon are registered trademarks of Sourcebooks, Inc.

All rights reserved. No part of this book may be reproduced in any form or by any electronic or mechanical means incl
ing information storage and retrieval systems—except in the case of brief quotations embodied in critical articles
reviews—without permission in writing from its publisher, Sourcebooks, Inc.

All activities in this book are to be conducted with appropriate adult supervision. Care must be taken by parents a
guardians to select activities that are appropriate for the age of the children. The authors and the publisher shall have
ther liability nor responsibility to any person or entity with respect to any mishaps or damage caused, or alleged to
caused, directly or indirectly by the information contained in this book.

All brand names and product names used in this book are trademarks, registered trademarks, or trade names of their resp
tive holders. Sourcebooks, Inc., is not associated with any product or vendor in this book.

Published by Sourcebooks, Inc.
P.O. Box 4410, Naperville, Illinois 60567-4410
(630) 961-3900
FAX: (630) 961-2168
www.sourcebooks.com

Originally published in 1995.

ISBN 1-4022-0535-X

The Library of Congress has catalogued the original edition as follows:
Ellison, Sheila.
365 days of creative play : for children two years and up / by Sheila Ellison and Judith Gray. — 3rd ed.
  p.   cm.
Includes index
1. Creative activities and seat work.   2. Amusements.   I. Gray, Judith Anne, date.   II. Title.
III. Three hundred sixty-five days of creative play.
GV1203.E363   1995
790.1'922—dc20   95-3261

Printed and bound in the United States of America.
VHG   10   9   8   7   6   5   4   3   2   1

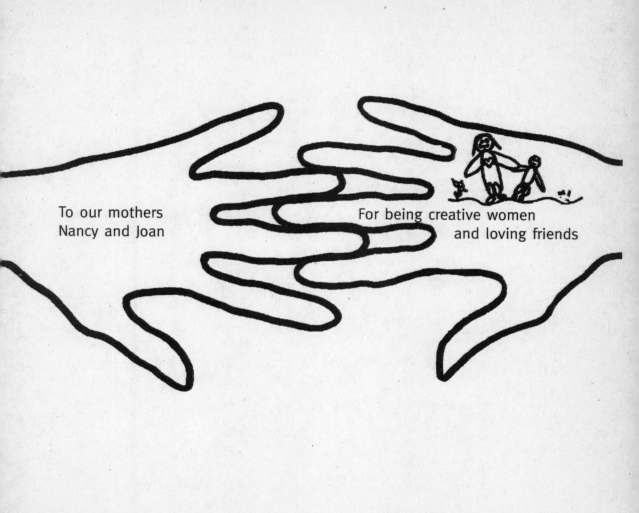

To our mothers
Nancy and Joan

For being creative women
and loving friends

Introduction

The early years greatly influence your child's development; how he or she interacts with the world, solves problems, and feels about him- or herself. Learning to play is as crucial as teaching your child to walk, talk, or read. Because play, in all of its many forms, provides parents and children with fun, interactive, positive experiences, which in turn lead to feelings of success and accomplishment. Creative play opens a space for imagination to grow, enhances parent/child relationships, and teaches important life skills through active participation.

This book will give you ideas of ways to spend magical time together. Included are sections on art, construction, craft, dance, education, environment, family, foods and cooking, games, horticulture, make-believe, music, and nature.

All the activities have been tried and tested by the authors, who would appreciate suggestions and comments from parents, teachers, and other readers. New ideas will be gratefully included in the next edition. Read, play, have fun, and enjoy!

For Your Child's Safety and Enjoyment

✓ Spread newspaper over and beneath working surface.

✓ Keep dangerous supplies out of reach or closely supervised.

✓ Dress your child appropriately for the activities—loose and old clothes are best.

✓ Carefully monitor the use of sharp tools and materials, such as scissors.

✓ Check outdoor areas for sharp objects before starting outside activities.

✓ Educate your child to recognize and avoid danger and harm.

✓ Clean your child's hands before cooking activities.

✓ Thoroughly wash and rinse brushes after use.

✓ Do not force your child to do the activities.

✓ Play with your child.

✓ Read carefully through the Materials and Directions before each activity.

✓ Adjust your time schedule—some activities take a few days, others a few minutes.

✓ The finished product or experience is less important than the process itself.

✓ Take this book with you while visiting or on vacation with your child.

✓ Allow your child to use his or her own creativity—he or she may see things differently.

✓ Other family members and friends may enjoy facilitating the activities.

✓ Above all, establish a nonthreatening, enjoyable play environment for all.

Materials and Supplies

Arts, Crafts, and Construction:

Crayons
Water-based pens or markers
Tempera paints
Paintbrushes
Construction paper
Pipe cleaners
String or twine
Paper cups and plates
Fabric and felt remnants
Ribbons and bows
Old magazines
Tissue paper
Newspaper
Thread spools
Corks and bottle caps
Glue or paste
Paper bags
Used boxes
Colored pencils
Colored chalk
Egg cartons
Watercolor paints
Yarn
Adhesive tape
Plaster of paris
Old shirts
Aluminum foil
Butcher paper
Scissors
Masking tape
Straws
Toothpicks

Foods and Cooking:

Vegetable food coloring
Assorted bowls
Cereals
Dried fruits
Grains
Pudding mixes

Music, Games, and Make-Believe:

Bed sheets
Sequins
Family photos
Dress-up clothes
Tapes and records
Cardboard cartons and boxes
Balls
Playing cards
Milk and oatmeal cartons
Plastic wrap
Cookie cutters
Baking pans
Rolling pin
Saucepans
Cookie sheet

Nature and Horticulture:

Potting soil
Pots—used, clay or plastic
Seeds
Glass jars
Popsicle sticks
Small handheld gardening tools
Fresh vegetables
Spring bulbs
Unbleached coffee filters

Table of Contents

Dance

Education

vironment

mily

Food

Games

Horticulture

Make-Believe

Music

Nature

Start here

art

yarn dog

Materials
1. Colored rug yarn or thick 8-ply knitting wool
2. Paper
3. White glue or glue stick
4. Dog photos or pictures
5. Cardboard

Directions
Trace a large clear picture of a dog onto the cardboard. This is just the basic outline, so don't worry about it looking exactly like the picture. Draw a mouth and eyes and outline the ears and tail. Cut the yarn or wool into one- or two-inch strands. Use an egg carton to separate the colors and to make selecting and handling of yarn easier. Show your child how to glue the yarn strands onto the dog outline, creating fur-like patterns. Once the dog is finished, give the dog a name and make up a story explaining how the dog came to have such brightly colored fur-like.

1

pavement painting

Materials
1. Plastic bucket
2. Large paintbrushes
3. Old sponges
4. Water

Directions

On a dry, warm day give your child a plastic bucket of water, one or two paintbrushes, and an old sponge. Find a safe driveway, wooden deck, cement wall, or stretch of pavement, and let her paint large pictures or patterns with the water onto the cement or wood surface. Pictures will dry and disappear, exciting your child with endless possibilities. Step into the bucket to make footprints, splash or drip water off fingertips. Use the sponges to press onto the hard surface or squeeze water into patterns.

connect the dots

Materials
1. Drawing paper
2. Pencil
3. Ink or ballpoint pen
4. Crayons or colored felt pens
5. Eraser

Directions
Using the pencil, make ten to thirty dots (depending on the counting ability of the child) on a plain sheet of drawing paper. Randomly number the dots in pencil with the first and last number on the same dot. Connect the dots in numerical order with the ink pen, creating an abstract drawing. Wait until dry and then erase the pencil numbers. Use crayons or felt pens to color in the design.

lacing cards

Materials
1. Greeting cards or postcards
2. Shoelaces—the longer the better
3. Hole punch
4. Glue

Directions

Glue the greeting card closed, or glue two postcards together. Allow time for the glue to dry. Punch holes around the edges of the cards. Make big holes for younger children and smaller holes for older children, according to the child's coordination. Let the child thread the shoelace through the holes. Make up different patterns; threading in one and out the other hole, or skipping a hole and then coming backwards.

pressed-flower place mats

Materials
1. Fresh flowers
2. Old phone book
3. Self-adhesive plastic

Directions

Open the book and lay the flowers between the pages. Repeat on other pages until there are no more flowers to press. Close the book and leave until the flowers are dry, checking every few days. Thin flowers will dry in a few days, thicker ones may take up to ten days. When the flowers are dry, remove carefully. Cut two pieces of plastic the general size and shape for your place mat design. You will trim to finished size, so don't worry about the pieces matching perfectly. Arrange the flowers on the plastic by holding carefully to each side then dropping them as flat as possible onto the plastic. The flowers will stick instantly, so some may be bent. This will add to the garden look, since many flowers are often seen from the side when growing in a group. Once all the dried flowers are stuck to the plastic, place the second piece of plastic on top (this will require adult help). Smooth out the wrinkles and trim the edges to the desired size.

painted soap

Materials
1. Bar of soap
2. Water-based paints
3. Small paintbrushes

Directions
Place soap on a sheet of newspaper. Mix paints and put colors in separate containers (paper cups). Let your child paint directly onto the soap with brushes or her fingers. Let the paint dry. The design can be readily washed off and your child can begin another one, or these soaps can be put on display in guest bathrooms before parties or special events. If you do the painting on aroma-rich soap, they can be placed in a bowl as room deodorizers.

crinkle crayon print

Materials
1. Crayons
2. Thick paper
3. Newspaper
4. Cold water
5. Paint—black or brown

Directions
Have your child draw a picture or design with the crayons on a sheet of paper. Crumple the paper and dip it into the water. Squeeze out the water and spread the drawing to dry on the newspaper. Paint over the drawing. Place another sheet of paper over the top immediately to soak up the excess paint. Separate the sheets of paper and your child will have a lithograph of the original drawing.

shell paintings

Materials
1. Seashells (chalkier white ones with
   a large, smooth inner surface work best)
2. Acrylic paints and brushes
3. Jar of fresh water

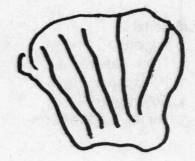

Directions
Rinse shells in fresh water. Let them dry. Paint the inside, letting each color dry before adding the next for a crisp, illustrated effect, or allow the paints to run together for a more modern look. Leave the shells out in the sun to dry. For a taste of summer in the middle of the winter, go to a craft store and buy shells. Turn the heat up in your house, put on bathing suits, lay an old sheet on the floor, and pretend to be on the beach painting shells.

art exploration

Materials
1. 1" or larger paintbrush, sponge, kitchen utensils
2. Large sheets of paper
3. Wooden spoons
4. Jar of water-based paint
5. Masking tape

6

Directions
Lay the paper on a flat surface and secure with tape. Show your child all the different ways to apply paint to paper—brushing, dabbing, flicking, and scraping. Encourage your child to experiment with a variety of applicators—brushes, sponge, spoons, and other kitchen utensils. Your child will explore not only the medium of art (paint) but also the tools that can be used to apply paint.

shadowy shapes

Materials
1. Large sheets of butcher paper
2. Crayons or felt markers
3. Finger paints

Directions
Go outside on a sunny day and have your child stand on the sidewalk or driveway while you quickly draw the outline of his shadow onto the butcher paper. Have your child put his body into interesting shapes and trace the outline again. When the outlines are complete, have your child paint them any way he wishes.

candle wax painting

Materials
1. Wax candle
2. Watercolor paper
3. Watercolors
4. Paint brush

Directions
Have your child draw a pattern or scene with the wax candle onto a sheet of watercolor paper. The drawing will be almost invisible. When finished, have your child paint the entire sheet with watercolors. When the paint dries, the original invisible drawing will show through.

flower-and-leaf prints

Materials
1. Fresh flowers and leaves
2. Unbleached muslin cloth
3. Paper bags or butcher paper
4. Hammer

Directions

Cover a table with paper bags or butcher paper. Spread out the fabric on top. Arrange the leaves and flowers in a design on half of the fabric. Fold the fabric so that the blank half is on top of the leaves and flowers. Feel where the flower and leaf outlines are against the fabric. Use a hammer and pound on the top of the leaves and flowers until the color has bled through the fabric. Make sure to go all the way to the edges or you will get a color with no shape. Open the fabric and scrape or peel off the plant residue. Experiment with which flowers work best. Use the fabric to make a pillow, place mat, bag, apron, or gift tags.

your coloring book

Materials
1. Crayons
2. Paper

Directions
Instead of buying a coloring book and having your child color in someone else's pictures, encourage her to make outlines for her own coloring book. Modern designs work best (the kind that don't look like anything specific). Once the outer design has been made in black, color in the inside. Collect the pictures in a binder.

swinging sand art

Materials
1. Sand
2. Large, strong paper cup
3. String
4. Large sheet of brown or colored paper
5. Liquid glue (optional)

Directions
This activity is best done outside. Make a hole in the bottom of the paper cup. Make another three holes around the rim. Suspend the cup from the string by threading the string through the holes and tying it to an overhang or branch. Spread the brown paper below. Now fill the cup with sand and gently push it so that it swings in small circles and arcs. The sand will pour out and make patterns on the paper below. Reuse the sand to repeat the activity. If you'd like to create a permanent design, dribble glue onto the paper in desired shapes before swinging the sand.

stone painting

Materials
1. Smooth, flat stones
2. Acrylic paints
3. Permanent markers
4. Paintbrushes
5. Jar of water

Directions
Clean and dry off the stones. Mix the paints and pour them into paper cups or muffin pans. If you are using tube paints, squeeze a little onto a plastic plate. Have your child paint the rocks in sequence—while the paint on one stone is drying, apply paint to the next stone. Continue until all the stones are colored and dry. Add lines and other designs with the pens. Use the water in the jar to wipe off mistakes and to clean brushes. Painted stones can be used as paper weights or ornaments.

moving masterpiece

Materials
1. Tempera paint
2. Newspaper
3. Large pieces of paper: butcher paper, newsprint, or wrapping paper
4. Ball: tennis ball, golf ball, or baseball

Directions
Choose an outdoor area that's easy to clean up: a patio, driveway, garage, or deck. Spread newspapers on the work surface, and place the paper on top. Put on old clothes. Set the ball in the paint and roll it around a little before setting it on the paper and rolling it to your child. Make sure you instruct your child to roll the ball on the paper, NOT throw it. It's also fun to dip the wheels of a favorite plastic or wooden vehicle in the paint and zoom it across the paper.

squashed paint art

Materials
1. Tempera paints
2. Drawing paper
3. Teaspoon
4. Rolling pin or wine bottle

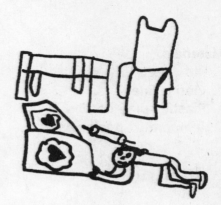

Directions
Put the paints in a muffin pan or paper cups. Take one sheet of paper and have your child dribble some paint onto it with the teaspoon. Cover this sheet with another sheet of paper. Use the rolling pin or wine bottle to squash the paint. Peel off the top sheet of paper and your child will have a double image of his or her artwork. Try this activity with several colors in different combinations. Make sure you don't drip the paint colors too close together or you may just get a mushy overlap. Vary the squashing techniques; use your fingers and rub over the paper softly, or roll in some places and tap your fingers in others.

sheet designs

Materials
1. Old sheet
2. Clothesline
3. Plastic spray bottles
4. Tempera or poster paint

Directions

Hang the sheet over a clothesline. Pour each color of tempera or poster paint into its own spray bottle, adding water until paint sprays easily (usually 50 percent water, 50 percent paint). Stand in front of the sheet and spray the paint in whatever design you want. If more than one person is participating, have each person take one color and spray together, creating a modern art overlapped effect. Let the sheet dry before taking it off the clothesline.

newspaper leaf prints

Materials
1. Assorted leaves
2. Saucers
3. Tempera or acrylic paints
4. Newspaper
5. Plastic soda bottle

Directions
Pour small amounts of paint into the saucers. Spread a sheet of newspaper on a flat surface. Dip each leaf in the paint and place it paint-side down on the newspaper. Repeat until several leaves are arranged on the paper. Cover arrangement with another sheet of newspaper. Use the soda bottle to roll over the top. Remove the top layer of newspaper. Carefully remove each leaf, and your child will have a set of colorful leaf impressions.

ancient scroll

Materials
1. Two chopsticks
2. Sheet of 8½" x 11" paper
3. Scissors
4. Tape
5. Colored pens
6. Yarn, cord, ribbon, or string

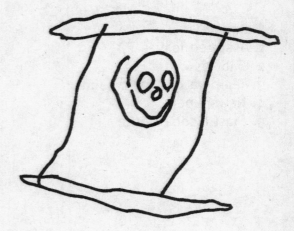

Directions
Trim the paper so that the chopsticks are two inches longer than the short side of the paper. Tape the chopsticks securely along each short side so that one inch protrudes at either end. Draw a picture and write a message on the paper. Roll up each side around the chopsticks until they meet in the middle. Tie a length of yarn around the scroll to keep it neat.

snow paintings

Materials
1. Spray bottles
2. Water
3. Food coloring

Directions
Use snow as your canvas and paint a museum masterpiece! Fill spray bottles with water and drops of food coloring (the number of drops determine how bright the painting will be). Spray the colored water onto the top of the snow to make the design of your choice.

chalky watercolor

Materials
1. Colored chalks
2. Drawing paper
3. Liquid starch
4. Paintbrush

Directions
There are two ways your child can make a chalk watercolor. The first way is to draw a picture with the chalks on the drawing paper and then brush liquid starch over it. The second way is to dip the paper in the starch to start, and then draw a picture with the chalks on the wet paper. Either way, when dry, these pictures look beautiful.

pot painting

Materials
1. Terra-cotta garden pot
2. Masking tape
3. Acrylic paints

Directions
Use the masking tape to make horizontal and/or vertical stripes along a terra-cotta garden pot. Let your child paint the pot with acrylic paints in whatever design she desires. Remove the tape when the paint dries and see how delighted she is to have created such tidy, symmetrical work.

Later, protect the painted finish from the elements with a coat or two of polyurethane varnish (if you plan to put the pot outside). These make great gifts, especially when you fill them with a favorite herb or flower.

transparent triumph

Materials
1. Newspaper
2. Drawing paper
3. Black felt marker
4. Crayons
5. Oil—baby or cooking
6. Rags

Directions
On the drawing paper, have your child outline a design or picture with the black marker. Color in parts of it with the crayons. Turn the drawing over and lay it face down on the newspaper. With the rag, rub oil on the back of the drawing paper. It will become instantly transparent. Hang the artwork in the window so the light can shine through.

watercolor contour

Materials
1. Drawing paper (watercolor paper is best)
2. Water-based paints
3. Cookie tray
4. Water
5. Paintbrushes

Directions
Fill the cookie tray with water. Dip a sheet of drawing paper in the water and hold it up to let the water drain off it. Lay it on some newspaper and while it is still wet, apply the paints with paintbrushes. Watch the blurring effect of the wet colors on the wet paper. When the paper is dry, your child can add detail with felt pens or crayons.

dip and dabble art

Materials
1. Paper towels or coffee filters
2. Muffin pan
3. Food coloring
4. Water

Directions
Mix the food coloring with some water in the muffin pan so your child has three or four colors to choose from. Fold the paper or filter any way your child wants, then dip the corners briefly into the colors. The paper will soak up the color. Fold again and stick the dry corner into the colored water. Let the paper dry before unfolding, otherwise it might tear. Experiment with different folds or try crumpling the paper before dipping it into the colors. Press the papers flat and mount on cardboard. Food color stains the fingers, so try to dip the paper, not the hands.

canvas rug

Materials
1. Piece of plain canvas
   (the size you want the rug)
2. Acrylic paint
3. Paintbrushes
4. Clear acrylic coating
5. Hot glue gun

Directions
Before your child begins to paint the rug, fold the edges over one inch and iron before securing with a hot glue gun. Put the acrylic paints onto a plastic plate and let your child paint the canvas. If there is a specific design he has in mind, pencil the design onto the canvas before starting. If you want to do a family rug, handprints are a good option. If mistakes are made, let the paint dry and then paint. After the paint is dry, cover the rug with a few coats of clear acrylic. Once the acrylic is dry, the rug can be sponged clean with soap and water.

customized light switch

Materials
1. Light switch plate
2. Acrylic paint
3. Small brushes

Directions

Replace your child's light-switch plate with a customized one that your child has created. Get all the materials ready. Using the small brushes, have your child paint on a design, picture, or her name. Wipe mistakes off with water, or wait until it dries and paint over the top of the dried paint. Let the plate dry completely before screwing it back on the wall.

object rubbings

Materials
1. Black, brown, or dark blue crayons
2. White drawing paper

Directions
Look around inside and outside with your child to try to find some textured surfaces on which to make rubbings. Small objects, such as coins, are good to start with. Later, try manhole covers, plaques, stucco, etc. Place the paper over the object and rub firmly back and forth with a crayon. An outline will soon appear. Rubbings can also be made of leaves, keys, woven baskets, and sidewalk cracks.

body beautiful

Materials
1. Large sheet of butcher or brown paper
2. Crayons or paints
3. Black felt marker
4. Scissors (optional)

Directions

Have your child lie down on the paper in any shapes she wants. Trace around the body with a felt marker. Have your child take over and draw her own features and clothes on the outline. It can be what she is actually wearing, or what she would like to be dressed in—a Halloween costume, for instance. The outline can be cut out or left on the large sheet and then hung up.

salt pictures

Materials
1. Salt
2. Dry tempera paints—in powder form
3. Drawing paper
4. Glue
5. Baby food jars

Directions
Mix the salt with the paint powder in a baby food jar, a separate jar for each color. Have your child either brush or dribble the glue to make patterns on the drawing paper. She may wish to spread the glue around more with her fingers. Now sprinkle the salt mixture over the paper using one or more colors. Wait until the glue dries and then tip off the excess colored salt. Make several pictures and hang the collection in the hallway.

contour line art

Materials
1. Drawing paper
2. Black felt pen
3. Crayons

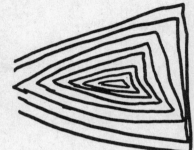

Directions

Have your child make a large, closed shape, such as a heart, box, ball, or triangle with the black felt pen. Starting on the inside near the shape's edge, repeat the outline. Continue redrawing it, getting smaller and smaller until it cannot be repeated. Now, color in each contour with different colored crayons. Don't worry if your child goes over the lines. This activity can also be done in reverse; start with a small shape and draw several outlines on the outside. If you want more space to color, draw the next line further from the one that has already been drawn.

picture paperweight

Materials
1. A smooth rock
2. Child's photo
3. Waxed paper
4. Tempera paint
5. Liquid glue
6. Paintbrush

Directions
Mix ¼ cup of tempera paint with ¼ cup of glue. Clean and dry rock and place it on waxed paper. Have your child paint the rock with the glue mixture. While still wet, carefully press the photo onto the rock. Let it dry completely before using as a paperweight.

karate string art

Materials
1. White paper
2. Tempera paints
3. Baby food jars or bowls
4. Strong string

Directions

Mix the paints and pour into jars. Cut the string into various lengths—six inches, nine inches, twelve inches, and eighteen inches. Tape paper down on a flat surface. Dip a length of string into paint and either drag or "karate chop" it onto the paper. Repeat with a different color. Cover the paper with color and line. When dry, the artwork can be used as a gift wrap or mounted and hung on a wall.

construction

homemade play dough

Materials
1. 1 cup salt
2. 1 cup flour
3. 1 cup water
4. Cookie cutters
5. Rolling pin or narrow bottle
6. Food coloring (optional)

Directions

Put salt and flour in a deep, unbreakable bowl. Drape an old shirt or smock on your child and allow him to mix the dry ingredients thoroughly with hands or a wooden spoon. Slowly add water (to which some drops of food coloring may have been added). Continue to mix, then knead dough until it is smooth and elastic without being sticky.

Dump the dough onto a flat, floured surface and roll it out with the rolling pin or bottle. Use cookie cutters to make shapes or provide your child with other cutting and poking utensils, such as plastic knives, bottle tops and lids, chopsticks, and assorted plastic shapes. Store in an airtight plastic container or Ziploc bag.

handprint plaque

Materials
1. Plaster of paris
2. Aluminum pie dish
3. Water
4. Nails
5. Food color (optional)

Directions

Prepare plaster of paris according to directions. When ready, pour a small amount into the greased pie dish. Lightly grease your child's hand and then press it gently into the center of the dish. Hold it there until the plaster sets—just a couple of minutes. Remove hand and let plaster set completely. A nail can be inserted while the plaster is still moist so the handprint can be hung on a wall. Also, try adding food color to the plaster mix at the start. Similar plaques can be made from footprints, elbows, and knees. Plaster of paris heats up as it mixes, so this step requires close adult supervision. Once the mold has cooled, try pressing play dough or molding clay into it to produce a replica of your child's hand.

cylinder sculpture

Materials
1. Construction paper
2. Fabric
3. Crayons
4. Buttons and beads
5. Yarn
6. Glue

Directions

Lay some paper flat on the table. Cover it with decorative ideas using fabric scraps, buttons, and beads. Attach firmly with glue. Fill in spaces with crayons. When paper is dry, roll it up into a cylinder shape. Glue or staple the ends together. Now stand it on one end and your child has made a cylindrical sculpture.

fluffy head

Materials
1. Large paper bag
2. White glue
3. Cotton balls
4. White tissue paper
5. Felt pen

Directions
Place paper bag over child's head and mark where his eyes and arm-holes are with a felt pen. Remove bag and use scissors to cut out the holes for eyes and arms. Place bag over the back of a chair so that you can walk around it while doing the activity. Dip cotton balls into a saucer of diluted white glue and then stick each one onto the bag. Scrunch pieces of tissue paper into balls or wads and glue them on top for ears, or elsewhere to cover gaps among cotton balls. When the entire bag is covered and the glue has dried, the child can wear it to play in.

boxes and buildings

Materials
1. Cardboard boxes
2. Masking tape
4. Paint (optional)

Directions
With the materials listed and some imagination, your child can build all kinds of objects and buildings from old boxes you were going to throw away. Here are some ideas—train, boat, car, spaceship, village, doll house, skyscraper, robot, or space station. Try creating a scene from a favorite story or use the buildings as a backdrop for a play.

39

streamer munchkin

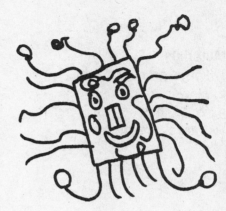

Materials
1. Large paper bag
2. White glue
3. Ribbons, yarn, colored string
4. Crayons
5. Colored paper

Directions
Place bag over your child's head and mark where his eyes and armholes are located with crayons. Remove the bag and cut out the holes for eyes and arms. Place the bag over the back of a chair to make decorating easy. Cut ribbons, yarn, paper, ribbons, and string into assorted lengths, not to exceed the child's height. Cover the front, back, and sides. When the glue is try, place bag over child's head and lead him in front of a mirror so he can see and admire the results.

grocery bag blocks

Materials
1. Large grocery bags
2. Newspaper
3. Wide masking or packaging tape

Directions
Lay the grocery bag on a flat surface and fold over the open edge, making a crease of two or three inches. Open the bag and fill with tightly crumpled newspaper. Fold the stuffed bag along the crease line and tape closed. Make several blocks this way until there are enough to build a fort, wall, or other imaginary structure. These blocks can be used indoors or outdoors and can be replaced with relative ease.

clay sculptures

Materials

1. Clay
2. Paintbrushes
3. Molding tools
4. Paints

Directions

Making things out of clay is a challenging and gratifying experience for children. Give your child a lump of ready-mixed clay and let her create any kind of object or shape. The first step will be to soften the clay by kneading it, pushing it against the table and squeezing it so that it will be easier to mold. Visit a local art supplier to get a little lesson in the types of clay that can be molded and then painted without firing. When the sculpted piece is completely dry (this could take a couple of days), your child can paint it.

wiggle worm

Materials
1. String or twine
2. Foam plastic egg carton
3. Toilet paper cardboard tubes
4. Scotch tape
5. Paints
6. Paintbrushes

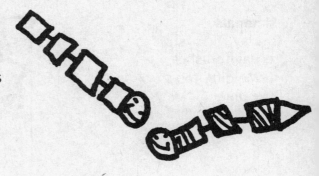

Directions

Paint the cardboard tubes with different colors and let them dry. Cut out two sections from the egg carton to be used for head and tail. Cut a length of string two and half feet long. Link the wiggle worm first by threading the string through one of the egg carton pieces, then through each of the tubes ending with a piece of egg carton for the tail. Make sure to leave at least a foot of string in front of the head for pulling your worm. Tie knots at both ends, then secure the string at the end to the egg carton tail with tape. Decorate the face. Pull the worm along and watch it wiggle and roll.

create a crown

Materials
1. Paper
2. Scissors
3. Glue
4. Crayons
5. Sparkles and glitter

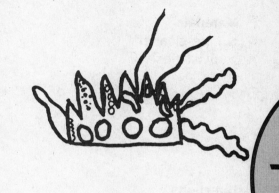

Directions
Cut the paper to look like an open crown shape. Let your child decorate it with crayons, glue, sparkles, and glitter. When the decoration is dry, fit it to your child's head and staple or glue the ends together. Play "king" or "queen" for a day and have your child wear the crown. Encourage your child to make more crowns for the entire family to be worn at the next family event.

pipe cleaner sculpture

Materials
1. Pipe cleaners
2. Twist ties

Directions
Help your child bend pipe cleaners into different shapes. Join some together and make more complex shapes. You can make people, animals, trucks, or anything you'd like. Join them together and hold them in the air, moving them back and forth. This is a fun family activity as you can make the sculpture as large as you'd like, with each person creating a mini-sculpture link at their own artistic ability.

45

wind sock

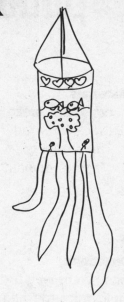

Materials
1. Cylindrical oatmeal or other cardboard container
2. Construction or contact paper
3. Tape, glue, or staples
4. Crepe paper or fabric strips

Directions
Remove the lid and cut off the bottom of a cylindrical container. Cover the box with construction or contact paper, and have your child decorate it with paint, markers, or glued bunches of paper. Together glue, tape, or staple crepe paper or fabric streamers to the inside of one end of the container. Punch four holes in the other end (across from one another). Tie one string, about twelve inches long, to two opposing holes, and another to the other two holes. Gather them both with a third, longer piece of string, which you will use to hang the wind sock. If possible, hang it outside a prominent window so your child will see it often.

make a sundial

Materials
1. 12" x 12" piece of heavy cardboard
2. Block of wood
3. Thumbtacks
4. Markers or paint

Directions

An ancient way to tell time was to use the sun and the shadows it casts. First, take the heavy cardboard and fold it corner to corner. Then cut the card in half. Fold a half-inch wide flap on the bottom of one card. Cut a twelve-inch circle out of the other piece of cardboard. Center the circle of cardboard over the block of wood and then put the triangle card on top of the circle. Attach the card to the circle of cardboard, pushing the thumbtacks through both pieces of cardboard into the wooden block. Make sure the triangle is straight up and down so it looks like a shark's fin sticking out of the circle. Place the sundial on a flat surface in the sun. Every hour, mark off where the shadow is cast. Using paint, markers, or crayons, decorate your sundial. Remember to keep the sundial facing the same direction so that your hour marks will be accurate.

log houses

Materials
1. Brown construction paper
2. Cardboard
3. Pencil
4. Tape
5. Glue

Directions

Cut the piece of cardboard the size you'd like the floor of your house to be. Cut the paper one inch longer and two inches wider than the house size. Wrap the paper around a pencil and tape it. Slide the log off the pencil and glue it to the cardboard floor, making sure that the end of the log sticks off the cardboard on alternating sides. Make your house as tall as you'd like it. When you're ready to start the roof, cut the logs accordingly. Add a cardboard roof once you have the logs assembled. You can also freeform any structure you'd like with the logs you've created, if you would like something other than a house.

tub sponge sculptures

Materials
1. Assorted sponges
2. Scissors
3. Water-resistant glue, such as Elmer's Stix-All

Directions
Cut the sponges into geometrical shapes. Involve your child in deciding which pieces to use to build interesting shapes: boats, ice cream cone, house, people, pets, or abstract sculpture. Glue the pieces together. Let the glue dry completely before playing with the shapes in the bathtub.

paper chains

Materials
1. Colored construction paper
2. Scissors
3. Glue, paste, or stapler

Directions
Cut paper into one-by-four-inch strips. Glue or staple the ends of the first strip to make a ring. Thread the next strip through this ring and glue the ends together. Continue threading the strips through the previous rings until the chain reaches the desired length, or you run out of paper. The chain can be used for holiday or birthday decoration.

room within a room

Directions

In a child's mind, even the smallest nook or cranny can become a hideaway, a fortress, or a teahouse. Create your child's own pint-sized private world, ripe for imagination and exploration—or even just an afternoon snooze. Use a corner of her room to erect a small fabric teepee (canvas over PVC pipe, wooden dowels, or even bamboo sticks from a garden shop work great) or a circus tent made out of a big, colorful sheet or parachute.

A playhouse can be fashioned from a giant appliance carton. Wallpaper or contact paper around the outside not only reinforces the cardboard structure (for hours of door- and window-opening play) but also allows you to personalize it to your child's interests. Add carpet remnants to the floor, toss in fluffy pillows, make windows for peeking in and out, and Velcro a play phone onto the inside wall. You'll "lose" your child for hours!

puffy fish

Materials
1. Paper bag used for lunches
2. Rubber band
3. Old newspaper
4. Markers or paints

52

Directions:
Stuff the bag with crumpled newspaper until it is half full. Wind the rubber band tightly around the middle of the bag. Fan out the open end of the bag to form the fish's tail. Paint or color the body and tail. Using the marker, draw eyes and a mouth. Create a way to attach fins! Several puffy fish can be constructed and hung in a group from the ceiling or a shelf.

self-portrait puzzle and gift

Materials
1. Large photo of your child (9" x 12")
2. Cardboard
3. Strong glue
4. Scissors

Directions
Cut the cardboard the same size as the photo. Glue the photo to the cardboard. Turn it over, and on the cardboard side, draw jigsaw puzzle lines—straight lines are easiest for younger children, curved for older. Cut along the lines. Let your child reassemble the pieces to form her own picture. Put puzzle pieces in a bag and give it to another family member to try. Send the puzzle to grandparents as a gift. Write a message on the back of the puzzle, if desired.

coat hanger mask

Materials
1. Wire coat hanger
2. Old nylon stocking
3. Fabric and felt scraps
4. Yarn
5. Glue

Directions
The adult will need to manipulate the coat hanger until it is in a rounded shape. Cut nylon stocking in half and pull lower (footed) half over the coat hanger. Tie around the neck with the yarn. Cut out eye and mouth shapes from fabric and felt pieces. Glue them onto the stocking. Make a few masks so you can act out different scenes. When finished, your child can hold the "mask" in front of her face and pretend to be the character depicted.

fancy dress hat

Materials
1. Hats—straw, felt, or fabric
2. Artificial flowers
3. Feathers and bows
4. Ribbons and old lace
5. Fabric remnants
6. Glue

Directions
Antique or thrift stores are a great place to look for old hats. Straw sun-hats also work well. Begin creating an interesting hat by covering the brim with fabric remnants and attaching them with glue. Next, attach the flowers, bows, and feathers. Wrap the ribbon and lace around the center and tie a bow in the back. Add more bits and pieces to the hat until the desired effect is achieved. Put on the hat and go find a mirror!

paddle boat voyage

Materials
1. Scrap block of wood: 4" x 8" x 2"
2. Thin strip of wood: 2" x 8" x ¼"
3. 2 long nails
4. Rubber band—small and thick
5. Hammer
6. Sandpaper

Directions
This activity requires an adult to help hammer or hold the wood steady while the child hammers. The wood can also be sanded smooth before beginning to avoid splinters. Hammer the two long nails into one end of the block of wood, just far enough so that they can't be pulled out. Test the rubber band to see that it stretches tightly across the nails. Place the thin strip of wood inside the rubber band and wind it round and round. The piece of wood is the paddle for the boat. Hold the paddle still while the boat is placed in the bathtub or sink. Release the paddle and watch the paddle boat move through the water.

cylinder city

Materials
1. Plywood or strong cardboard
2. Paper cylinders—all sizes
3. Paints and paintbrushes
4. Scissors
5. Masking tape or glue

Directions
You are creating a city of cylinders standing upright like skyscrapers. Cut some of the cylinders in half, thirds, and fourths to increase the range of sizes and shapes of the cylinder collection. Paint or decorate the cylinders before attaching them to the cardboard. Dip one end of each cylinder in glue and set on the cardboard or plywood. Hold until the cylinder is stable, or use masking tape to tape the cylinders upright. Your child should make all the decisions about where each cylinder should be placed. Allow all the cylinders to dry. Give your city a name, state, and zip code.

pinwheels

Materials
1. Paper
2. Long dressmaking pin
3. Penny
4. Pencil with eraser or cardboard hanger tubes
   (used by drycleaners)
5. Crayons or felt pens

Directions
Cut the paper into a square shape—six inches by six inches. If using plain paper, now is the time to apply decorations with crayons or felt pens. Draw diagonal lines, corner to corner. Trace around a penny in the center of the diagonal lines. Remove penny and then cut along the diagonals from each corner to the edge of the circle in the center. Fold (without creasing) each corner into the center and fasten together with the pin. Stick the pin firmly into the top of the eraser of the pencil or cardboard tube top. Hold the pinwheel in the wind or run with it, and watch how it spins.

cork sculptures

Materials
1. Corks of different sizes and shapes
2. Glue
4. Paints and paintbrushes

Directions
Glue corks together to make familiar or imaginary shapes. Wait until glue dries. If your child wants to play with the sculptures in the bath-tub, there is no need to paint them. Otherwise, apply colorful paints and wait until completely dry before using them.

tugboat

Materials
1. A quart milk carton
2. Empty wooden matchboxes
3. Tube from toilet paper roll
4. Glue

Directions

Cut the milk carton in half, lengthwise, to make the boat bottom (hull). Glue two of the matchboxes together to make the cabin. Glue the toilet paper roll to the back of the cabin to make the smokestack. Finally, glue the cabin and smokestack onto the bottom of the boat. See if it will float in the bathtub.

plaster box etchings

Materials
1. Plaster of paris
2. Oil or Vaseline
3. Aluminum pan
4. Nails
5. Paints and paintbrushes
6. Damp cloth or sandpaper

Directions
Mix plaster of paris according to directions and pour into a pan. Let it set until quite dry and firm. Once hard, turn it out onto a paper-covered flat surface. Use the nails and other sharp objects to scratch or carve a design or picture into the dried plaster of paris. Lightly brush paint over the etched surface and wait until it dries. Using a damp cloth or sandpaper, remove the surface paint until only the colored etching is exposed. Prop up the finished etching on a shelf or mantelpiece for everyone to see.

picture frames

Materials

1. Cardboard from a carton
2. Fabric remnants
3. Glue or paste
4. Thumbtacks
5. Markers or paint

Directions

Remove the bottom of a cardboard carton. Cut the fabric several inches larger than the size of the cardboard frame. Miter the corners to fit. Attach the fabric to the cardboard with glue, stretching it to make a smooth surface and attaching the fabric to the outer sides of the cardboard. Decorate any cardboard that remains uncovered by fabric.

Let the glue dry before mounting the child's artwork with thumbtacks. For a permanent frame, glue the artwork directly onto the fabric.

tennis ball puppet

Materials
1. Tennis ball
2. Cloth napkin or men's handkerchief
3. Paints, crayons, or markers
4. Thumbtacks (optional)

Directions
Cut a hole in the base of the tennis ball big enough for the child's finger. Make the tennis ball into a face with paints, crayons, and markers. Use thumbtacks for eyes. Glue on yarn or colored paper for hair. Place the napkin over the child's hand and have him insert his or her index finger into the tennis ball base. The child's thumb and middle finger will be the puppet's arms. Attach the napkin to the "arm" fingers with a loose rubber band. Now the puppet is ready for action.

crafts

fabric garden

Materials
1. Scraps of plain and floral fabric
2. White glue or glue sticks
3. Poster board
4. Pictures of flowers (optional)

Directions
Cut out flower shapes from the fabric: petals, leaves, stems, and buds. An adult can do the cutting of shapes if the child is too young. If you have a group of children or family who would like to do this project together, use a roll of butcher paper instead of the poster board, and give each artist a place on the butcher paper to create their section of the group garden. Glue the shapes onto the poster board to make individual flowers, imaginary flora, a flower garden, or field of flowers. Try creating flower people or fairies, drawing a face where the center of a flower would be. Stems can resemble dancing legs, and leaves can turn into arms.

penny can

Materials
1. Plastic or metal cylinder with a plastic fitted lid
2. Assorted stickers, stamps, and gummed labels
3. Masking tape
4. Colored markers

Directions
Completely cover the outside of the cylinder with stickers, stamps, and labels. Use white glue to attach, if necessary. Make a small slit in the plastic lid big enough for coins to fit through. Put the lid on and tape it down securely. Use colored markers to decorate or conceal the tape. There will be more incentive to save pennies when the "bank" has been self-constructed. When the can begins to fill, open a bank savings account so your child can deposit his coins.

accordion paper people

Materials
1. Pencil
2. Paper
3. Scissors
4. Crayons

Directions
Fold paper, accordion-fashion, in three-inch strips so that all sections are equal. The number of folds in the paper determines the number of people in the chain. On the top piece of the folded paper, draw a person whose hands extend to touch the folds of the paper on each side. Carefully cut around the person, making sure NOT to cut where the hands meet the folds. Open up the paper and your child will have a chain of several people holding hands. Color them in with crayons, make different expressions on each face, or create a themed group. Kids enjoy creating a replica of their family, so make sure you have enough folds to include whoever your child would like in the family group.

stringy gift wrap

Materials
1. White newsprint paper
2. Water-based paints (tempera)
3. Toilet paper cardboard tubes
4. Newspaper
5. Thick string
6. Muffin pan
7. Paintbrushes

Directions
Place several colors of paint in a muffin pan with a separate paintbrush for each color. Stuff each cardboard tube full of newspaper to make it stronger. Wind the string around paper tubes, taping the ends into the end of the tube. Spread the paper on a flat surface and stabilize with tape. Paint the string on the tubes, and while still wet, roll the tube over the paper until paint is used up. Repaint string with another color and roll again. When finished rolling, wait until the paint is completely dry before removing paper and using it as gift wrap.

yarn holder

Materials
1. Wide cylindrical container with a plastic lid
2. Colored yarn
3. Double-sided cellophane tape

Directions
Wrap tape around the outside of the can starting at the top—but only do a couple of rows at a time. Take pieces of yarn and wind them around the container, pressing into the sticky tape. Repeat until the container is completely covered with rows of yarn. Punch one or more holes in the lid, depending on the size of the can. Place a ball or hunk of yarn inside the container and draw the end(s) through the hole(s) in the lid. Replace the lid. If the yarn is to be used for knitting, additional holes can be made for knitting needles.

felt storyboards

The beach was fun we could see many boats

story

Materials
1. Colorful pieces of felt or flannel fabric
2. Shoe box lid or piece of strong cardboard
3. Glue
4. Sandpaper
5. Photographs or magazine cutouts

Directions
Cut the piece of felt or flannel large enough to cover the inside of the box lid or over the piece of cardboard. Glue the fabric to the cardboard. Cut out pieces of felt in the shape of people, animals, trees, cars, spaceships, or whatever you want to tell a story about. Objects made of pieces of felt will naturally stick to the background fabric. If you want to use pictures from magazines or photographs, cut out the picture, then glue it to a piece of cardboard of the same shape. Glue sandpaper to the back so it will stick to the felt board. Tell a story. As each character is mentioned, attach it to the felt board. Or put a few shapes up on the board and ask your child to make up a story.

smoothie gift wrap

Materials
1. Thick, white paper (butcher paper works well)
2. Water-based paints (tempera)
3. Spoons
4. Cling wrap
5. Muffin pan or paper cups

Directions
Mix and pour paints into a muffin pan or paper cups. Spread paper onto a flat surface and tape it down to keep it stable. Using spoons, dribble and drip paint onto paper, experimenting with different colors. While still wet, place a layer of cling wrap over the paint covering the whole surface. Use hands to smooth cling wrap and create "smoothie" designs underneath. Carefully peel off the cling wrap and allow paper to dry completely before using as gift wrap.

bottle to vase

Materials
1. Bottles or other glass containers that could be used as a vase
2. Colored tissue paper
3. Scissors
4. Photographs copied onto paper or colored pictures from magazines
5. Brush
6. Glue or Mod Podge (found at craft stores)

Directions
Cut or tear the tissue paper into pieces. Mix glue with water (two parts glue to one part water) and brush a thin layer of the mixture onto the bottle. Carefully attach the pieces of tissue paper and photographs to the bottle. Continue until the whole bottle is covered. If you don't want to use any photographs, the vase looks just as pretty using only colored tissue paper. Once dry, brush over the tissue paper and photographs with the glue mixture. Let it dry completely before using it as a vase. Other objects, such as small boxes, can be decorated in the same way and used to store small toys or trinkets. Photographs must be copied onto paper in order for them to be flexible enough to stick and for the finish not to run.

object outline

Materials
1. Household items with flat bases
2. Large sheet of paper
3. Crayons or felt pens

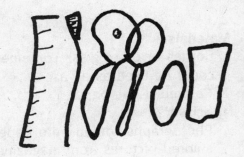

Directions
Spread the sheet of paper on the floor and tape it down. Send your child to search the house for objects with simple, distinct forms. Place the object on the paper and have your child trace around its base with a crayon or felt pen. Repeat with more found objects until the paper has an interesting design of overlapping outlines. You may need to hold the object while your child draws the outline so it doesn't slip under the paper.

lamp shades

Materials
1. Inexpensive, plain cardboard lamp shades
2. Felt-tipped markers or paint markers
3. Paint
4. Old fabric
5. Glue
6. Fringe

Directions
Put out the possible decoration supplies and let your child decide on how the lamp shade will be decorated. If you plan to put it in a bedroom, you might want to talk about color schemes, or put out only the paint or fabric that would match the room.

texture casts

Materials
1. Modeling clay or play dough
2. Shoe box

Directions
Work the clay or play dough into several smooth, flat shapes—like pancakes. Now go around the house and make imprints of different surface textures. Press the clay or play dough into the surface and then peel it off to see the imprint. You may want to walk around with your child to make sure the surface he is taking an imprint of will not be damaged by the dough. Save the imprints and play a guessing game. Look at all the imprints and try to identify the surfaces: a sole of tennis shoe, a floor mat, an outside wall, or a tennis racquet. This game is fun to play with kids or adults who were not around when the imprints were made.

make a snake

Materials
1. Paper plate
2. Crayons or markers
3. Scissors
4. Red yarn or construction paper
5. Glue

Directions
Using crayons or markers, completely cover both sides of the paper plate with colorful designs—stripes, circles, zigzags, and lines, for example. Starting at the outer edge, cut the plate into a spiral until the center is reached. This small, center circle will become the snake's head. On the head, draw eyes and then glue on a small strip of red paper (or use the yarn) to make a tongue. Hold on to the snake's head and the snake's body will uncoil.

learning mats

Directions

Find or buy a carpet remnant at least four feet by six feet. Use stencils to paint numbers, time tables, letters, foreign words, or other designs, depending on what your child is learning at the time.

Make a hop-scotch pattern, a huge checkerboard, or big, open shapes to be used as part of an obstacle course. Play musical hop by turning on music while your child runs around the rug. When you stop the music and yell out a number, letter, design, or shape, the child has to run to that location and do a little dance. You can make up all sorts of games to play on your learning mat.

miniature house

Materials
1. Small, cardboard box and flat cardboard pieces
2. Scraps of felt, fabric, and lace
3. Wallpaper remnants
4. Odds and ends to make furniture
   (matchboxes, spools, etc.)
5. Glue
6. Stapler

Directions
Divide the box into two rooms by cutting the additional cardboard and wedging it into the box. Line the walls with fabric or wallpaper. Cover the floors with felt or furry fabric. Make small pieces of furniture out of matchboxes, spools, or cardboard. Draw the windows and doors with felt pens and carefully cut them out. Add lace curtains by gluing or stapling. Continue decorating and furnishing until the miniature house is ready for some inhabitants.

photo mobile

Materials

1. Photos
2. 6" x 24" strip of thick, light-colored paper, or poster board
3. Scissors, string, stapler
4. Crayons, felt-tip pens

Directions

Take the strip of paper or poster board and evenly divide it into the number of pictures you plan to draw, or photos you will attach. Color or decorate in between the pictures. Curve the strip around in a circle and staple it so you have an open circle with pictures or drawings on the outside. Take three pieces of string of equal length and attach them to the top of the cylinder in three evenly spaced spots. Tie the strings together at the top and hang.

colored crayon balls

Materials
1. Old and broken crayons
2. Used plastic sandwich bags
3. Twist ties
4. Muffin pans

Directions
Peel the paper off the old crayons and break them into small pieces. Select a group of several different colors and place them in the sandwich bag. Seal tightly with a twist tie. Put several bags of crayon pieces in the muffin pan. Place the pan in the sun or in a slightly warm oven for twenty minutes or until the crayon wax is soft. It should never be hot. With the crayons still in the bags, shape them into balls. Drop the bags into ice-cold water. Remove the firm balls from the bags and use them to color.

egg carton insects

Materials
1. Egg carton
2. Paint
3. Hole punch
4. Pipe cleaners
5. Googly eyes (buy at craft store)

Directions
Cut the egg carton into sections. Paint and decorate each section according to whatever critter you are trying to create. Glue on the googly eyes. Punch a hole for the mouth. Depending on how many legs and how long they will be, cut the pipe cleaners accordingly. Punch a hole into the cardboard with a paper clip for each leg and push the pipe cleaner through it, twisting it into place. If your insect has antennae, punch a hole through the top and thread the pipe cleaners through, twisting them into antennae.

my life book

Most kids experience time in child care of some sort, whether it be a daycare center, baby-sitter in the home, or time with relatives or friends. Make the transition easier by creating a book full of photos of your child's everyday life and activities. Take pictures of their pets, yard, friends, car, toys, and common things they like to do. Let the person caring for your child know about the book so they can sit down with your child and let him tell the story of his life. Bring the book with you on any trip away from home.

spoon people

Materials
1. Plastic spoons
2. Cotton balls
3. Pipe cleaners
4. Felt pens
5. Construction and tissue paper
6. Scissors and glue

Directions
To make little people or puppets out of the plastic spoons, first glue on the cotton balls for hair and/or a beard. Twist pipe cleaners around "neck" of spoon to form arms. Use felt pens to draw on facial features. Finally, create clothing from the paper, attaching with yarn or string. Collaborate with your child to produce a story or play with the spoon people as characters.

cork boats

Materials
1. Assorted corks
2. Straws
3. Toothpicks
4. Lightweight paper

83

Directions

Cut the corks in half, creating a flat underside. Cut sails from the paper and use the toothpicks as masts. Make sure to have plenty of spare dry paper sails because if the sails are wet, the boat will tip over. Attach the sails by poking the toothpicks through the paper. Set the cork boats in water so that they sail upright. Propel the boats along by blowing through the straws. If using a large bowl of water, conduct races to see who can blow their boat from one side to the other.

bag lady doll

Materials
1. Paper grocery bags
2. Construction paper
3. Crayons
4. Yarn
5. Pieces of fabric

Directions
Lay one of the bags flat and have your child draw her version of a doll's face. Glue or staple several lengths of yarn to form hair. Use fabric pieces or colored paper to make a bow or turban for the hair. Cut strips of paper from one of the other bags to make arms and legs and glue these to the "face" bag. More fabric can be used for feet and hands. Attach these with glue or staples. Construct and add other accessories from fabric or construction paper. Name your doll as you make up a story about the bag doll's life.

papier-mâché balloon

Materials

1. Newspaper
2. Balloon
3. Flat dish or pan
4. Paints and paintbrushes
5. Paste—wallpaper or wheat
6. Yarn or rubber band

Directions

Mix the paste until it is thin and creamy, then pour a little into a flat pan. Tear the newspaper into narrow strips six to eight inches long. Have lots and lots of them. Blow up the balloon and tie it tightly with the yarn or rubber band. Dip the newspaper strips in the paste and apply to the outside of the balloon. Cover the balloon completely and then repeat with two or three more layers. Smooth the surface with your hands and wipe off any excess paste. Allow the paper to dry completely for a day before decorating with paint and paintbrushes.

career paper dolls

Materials
1. Cardboard
2. Construction paper
3. Scissors
4. Glue
5. Crayons

Directions
Adult should first trace or draw some different body shapes onto the cardboard—male and female. Add facial features and hair. Discuss with your child the different careers or jobs that people have. Then let him decide which ones will apply to the cardboard shapes. Using construction paper, scissors, and glue, outfit the cardboard dolls appropriately. For example: dancer, chef, doctor, builder, or farmer.

3-D picture frame

Materials
1. Paper grocery bag
2. Coat hanger
3. 9"x 12" photo of child or other family member
   (could also use a piece of your child's artwork)

Directions
Turn paper bag upside down. Cut a square or round opening in the bag about a foot down from the base. Cut another small hole in the center of the base to hang the hanger on. Tape the photo to the inside of the larger opening and check to see that it is visible and lined up. Take the coat hanger and put it inside the bag. Pull the curved handle through the smaller hole and hang the three-dimensional frame somewhere where it can be seen.

life-size me in PJs

Materials
1. Brown wrapping paper or plain newsprint
2. Felt marker
3. Scissors
4. Paints and thick paintbrushes

88

Directions
Roll out paper and tape it down on the floor. Have your child lie down on the paper on her back or front pretending to be asleep. Trace around the outline of the child's body with a felt marker. When the child gets up, suggest that she paint on the outline as if she were going to bed. Draw and color pajamas, slippers, nightdress, and perhaps a favorite bedtime toy. When finished, cut out the outline and tape to the back of the bedroom door or above the bed.

bean bag buddies

Materials
1. Old mitten
2. Felt and fabric pieces
3. Glue (for attaching fabric)
4. Dried beans or rice

Directions
Decorate mitten with cutout shapes from felt and fabric pieces. Mitten can be made to look like an animal, person, or abstract design. Glue felt or fabric shapes on securely. Fill the mitten with a handful of dried beans or rice. Have an adult stitch up the opening of the glove so that none of the beans or rice can escape. Bean bag buddies can be cuddled, tossed, or played with.

fabric weaving

Materials
1. Large fabric scraps or pieces
2. Scissors
3. Piece of cardboard or Styrofoam
4. Thumb tacks

Directions
Before your child starts weaving, cut a large square out of fabric—canvas or a heavy-weight fabric—which will create the frame your child will weave the thin strips of fabric in and out of. Leave an inch or two around the outside edge and then cut lines about three inches apart inside the square all going in one direction. Use the thumbtacks to loosely secure the piece of fabric to the cardboard. Take the remaining fabric and cut narrow strips out of it. Give these strips to your child and show him how to weave them in and out of the square. After the square is completely woven, stitch around the edge with a sewing machine to prevent unraveling. Use as a doll's blanket or place mat.

picture magnets

Materials
1. Magnetic tape (found at office supply
   or craft stores)
2. White unlined index cards
3. Markers, paints, crayons
4. Photographs, magazine pictures and words

Directions
Cut the index card in the shape of the magnet. Look at the picture you plan to glue on it to get ideas for shapes; if you're doing an animal collage, perhaps a dog bowl; a winter theme might be in the shape of a sled. Decorate the index cards before gluing on the pictures. Write captions or glue on words from magazines in collage style. Glue the magnetic strip onto the back.

clothespin hang-ups

Materials
1. Poster board
2. Spring-type wooden clothespins
3. Paints and paintbrushes
4. Glue
5. Yarn
6. Hole punch

Directions
Cover work area with newspapers. Mix paints and pour into muffin pans or paper cups. Punch holes in upper corners of poster board. Paint over poster board until all or most of it is covered. While the poster board is drying, paint the clothespins too. When the clothespins are dry, glue them onto the poster board. Let the glue dry and then thread some of the yarn through the holes in the clothespins that are next to each other. Tie yarn leaving a loop between clothespins. Now your child has a bulletin board on which to hang things and clip papers. Attach the poster board to a wall via the punched holes.

snowman alive

Materials
1. Paper grocery bag
2. Cotton balls (white)
3. White tissue paper
4. Glue
5. White Styrofoam

Directions
Place the bag over your child's head and mark where his eyes and arms are located. Remove the bag and cut out holes for eyes and arms. Put the bag over the back of a chair for decorating. Paint the bag white, if desired. Dip cotton balls into a saucer of glue and attach them to the paper bag. Scrunch up small pieces of the tissue paper and do likewise. Dip Styrofoam pieces into glue and add them too. Continue until the bag is totally covered. Mound extra balls of tissue onto the top of the bag to give a rounded look. Wait until the glue dries before the child wears the snowman costume and acts out a snowman story.

dance

let's move!

Directions:
At an early age, children associate how they move to words that describe the movements they make. For example: run, lie down, stand up, walk. This activity will help your child build his movement vocabulary.

Practice the following basic movement words and explore the variations with your child:
WALK—forwards, backwards, sideways, on tiptoe, very fast, slowly.
RUN—in circles, with small steps, lifting the knees, without using arms.
JUMP—in place, feet together, feet apart, forwards, backwards, sideways.
HOP—in a circle, changing feet, in place, while counting, sideways.
GALLOP—forward, fast, changing direction, changing feet.
LEAP—run and leap, with arms high, over an object or a line, high.
SKIP—softly, with a partner, high, in circles, with long steps, in place.

clockwork marching

Directions

In this activity, your child will march to a steady beat—a metronome is ideal, or you can clap your hands. Ask your child to march to the beat, swinging his arms wide and lifting his feet high for slow beats, short and low for faster beats. Try slowing down the beat and also making it faster. See how your child adjusts his or her marching to the tempo changes. When the beat stops, stop marching. Let your child create the rhythm while you march. Try marching together to a song with a strong drum beat. Then, stop marching while the song goes on and continue to clap the beat that you were walking to, then resume marching in time with the music. It's also fun to count the beats together, or count to ten and then start over.

action words

Directions

Introduce these words to your child and both of you do the actions together—STRETCH, LEAP, SLIDE, RUN, CRAWL, FALL, SPIN, and TURN. Once your child understands what each word means and how to do the action, put on music and try them out. Call out each word and do the action a few times together, then call out a number before the action (for example, "three leaps") and perform the movement called out. Make dances using two or three of the words in a row: run, turn, slide. Vary the directions and levels—do the action word backwards or sideways, low to the ground, or stretched high in the air.

rubber-neck dance

Directions
While facing your child, identify all the parts of the face and neck that can move: wiggle your nose, raise your eyebrows, stretch your neck, and stick out your tongue. Now sit in front of a mirror with some rhythmic music on and suggest how a face can dance by moving features in time with the music. Experiment with repeated facial expressions; from smile to frown in rhythm. Move your head from side to side stretching and turning the neck. Even hair can dance with a little help from little fingers.

fireworks dance

Directions
Have a discussion with your child about the shapes and sounds of fireworks and about his or her reactions to fireworks displays. Move with your child and shoot into the air with a loud sound, then drift down to the ground making a soft sound. Alternate jumping, leaping, and exploding loudly, and then landing quietly. Try jumping, leaping, and exploding quietly with loud landings. As a finale, do a dance showing many fireworks going off, one after the other.

freeze and melt

Directions

Have your child run freely around the space. When you say "freeze" or clap your hands, she must stop and remain absolutely still. When you say "melt," your child can relax and start to move around again. Continue freezing and melting in various shapes. Let your child say "freeze" and "melt" while you move around the room. Be creative with the shapes you choose to become.

mirror dancing

Directions
Depending on the size of the mirror, stand or sit in front of one with your child beside you. You can pretend you are on TV. First, start dancing with the face and head, moving eyes, noses, and eyelashes. Then add the shoulders and neck. Continue to dance with other body parts, watching how you both look in the mirror. You might like to try a duet with both of you doing the same thing while looking in the mirror. Turn and face each other so that you become the mirror for each other. One person does the movements and the other copies, reflecting the movements back like a mirror. Switch roles.

walk like the animals

Directions

In this dance activity, your child will try to simulate the ways animals move. Start with familiar animals—cat, dog, duck, and lizard, for example. Say, "If you were a cat, how would you come towards me?" or, "If you were a lizard, how would you move away from me?" Avoid telling your child to move like a certain animal. Instead, allow him to sense and create the movements from within. Watch a show or visit a zoo or aquarium to see how animals move about in their natural environments. After your child has a chance to move like a particular animal, ask him to describe how he was moving.

wiggle-waggle dance

Directions
Play some rhythmic music. Ask your child to warm up his body by wiggling every part. This can be done standing, sitting, or on the floor. After wiggling for a minute, ask your child to NOT wiggle a certain body part, such as the head. Continue to eliminate body parts until only the toes are wiggling. Repeat this activity, but this time start with one body part wiggling and gradually add all the other parts. Cool down.

balloon dance

Directions

Attach air-inflated balloons to short lengths of string. Have your child hold the balloon away from her body and move around it, trying not to get too close. Still holding the string, toss the balloon into the air and let it float down. Follow the movement the balloon is making by going upwards when the balloon is tossed and downwards as the balloon floats down. Holding the string, do turning and wave-like movements with the balloon. Turn on some music and create a dance with the balloon.

yoga toad

Directions
Practice this activity with your child until you both perfect it. Squat on your heels and balance. Put the palms of your hands on the floor. How long can you balance there? Help by holding your child's hips up. Take small hops forward keeping the arms touching the inner knees or thighs. Avoid putting stress on the knees.

tightrope walker

Directions

For this activity, your child will imagine he or she is a tightrope walker in a circus. Choose a crack in the sidewalk or a seam in a floor to be the "rope." Imagine that it is important to keep your balance and hold arms out wide. Walk on tip-toe forwards, backwards, and sideways. Try turning on the "rope" and balancing on one foot. The important thing is not to fall off!

bridges and tunnels

Directions

First, discuss with your child the differences between bridges and tunnels—what they typically look like and what they are used for. Make a bridge with your body and have your child go over it. Next make a tunnel and have your child go through it. Take turns creating interesting bridges and tunnels. If there are other children, you can make a series of bridges and tunnels and have the children go over and through them.

elephant stomp

Directions

Ask your child to describe the characteristics of an elephant: size, strength, weight, and shape. Ask your child to show you how a big heavy elephant would move. How would it turn around? How would it get down onto the ground and roll over? Make sure your child is acting out each response and not just answering in words. The goal is to become the elephant; think, move, and thunder while walking. How does an elephant move in a hurry? Would an elephant grab an apple with his trunk or mouth from an apple tree? What does a tired elephant do?

touch twister

Directions
Identify body parts with your child: knees, elbows, neck, fingers, toes, wrist, ankles, and nose. Choose a part and then try to touch another body part with it; hand to heel, nose to knee, or heel to bottom. Do this activity together. Touch a body part of yours with one of your child's; head to back, elbow to elbow, ear to shoulder. Enjoy the touching, twisting, and learning.

high space, low space

Directions

Go outside with your child and talk together about the space around us. Distinguish between "high" space up in the sky, "low" space (down on the ground), and "medium" space (in the middle). What living things move in these spaces? Ask your child how she would move in a high space (like a bird), in low space (crawling like a bug or snake), and middle space (animals with four legs). Experiment with dance movements exploring the space above and below.

space dance

Materials
1. Balls or balloons
2. Electronic music
   (e.g., "The Planets" by Horst)

Directions
For this activity, children represent the sun, moon, and planets, and imagine they are in space above and around the Earth. Using balls or balloons of different sizes or their arms in round shapes, they move around each other turning and spinning. This activity is an opportunity to learn about rotation and revolution and the names of familiar planets. Children can also imagine they are satellites, spaceships, flying saucers, and astronauts. Play the music as a celestial background.

rope shaping

Directions

Find a jump rope or a length of cord. Make a simple shape with it on the floor. Ask your child to move his body into the same shape. Repeat by making other interesting shapes with the rope. Now reverse the order of the activity. Have your child make a shape and then try to duplicate it with the rope. This is a good activity for other family members to join in, since sometimes it takes two people to imitate the shape of the rope.

leggy dance

Directions

Play some bright, rhythmical music. Stand facing your child and point out the different parts of the legs and feet. Now discover all the ways each part can move: bend the knees, wiggle the toes, circle the ankles, arch the foot, kick, and hop. Dance on one leg and dance with both legs. Add other body parts when child is ready—head, arms, shoulders, back, and waist.

silly walks

Directions

First of all, ask your child to walk around in her normal, everyday walk. Now try walking very high, very low, very wide, very narrow, very fast, and very slowly. Think of other ways people walk and try them out. Now ask your child to create her own special walk and make it as silly as possible. Can you do your silly walk backwards? Sideways? Turning? Finally, slow down your silly walk until it stops in an unusual shape. Next time you are out in public, sit and enjoy watching how unique each person's walk can be.

circle dancing

Directions

Identify with your child all the things in and around the house that are circular. These may include wheels, plates, balls, clock faces, coins, cookies, and doorknobs. Roll a coin and a ball and watch them travel. Have your child put his body into a round or circular shape. Encourage your child to move in circles and explore the ways round objects move in place and from place to place. Try spinning and swirling too.

inside-outside moves

Directions

Illustrate the difference between inside and outside with a box. Have your child get inside and explore the movements that are possible. Next have your child move outside the box, staying close to it. Alternate between inside moves and outside moves. Try moving only the hands inside the box, then only the hands outside the box. Repeat with feet, head, and one leg. Finish with all parts in or all out. If your child is at all claustrophobic with the idea of being inside a box, have her imagine a bubble and pretend to be touching the inside or outside of it.

abc shapes

Directions

Review the letters of the alphabet that your child knows and recognizes. Start with the most familiar letter of the alphabet and have your child make the shape of the letter with his body. It helps to show your child a picture or an example of the letter first. This is a good activity with another child, since many letters need two bodies to complete.

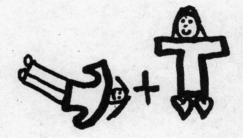

if toys could dance

Directions

Ask your child to collect a few of her favorite toys. Set them down with you and your child and talk about what would happen if each toy could move and dance. How would they dance? Let your child show you how each of her toys might move. Alternatively, ask your child, "If you were that toy, what kind of dance would you do?"

body sculpting

Directions
Ask your child to pretend that he is a soft lump of play dough and that you are the sculptor. Gently move your child's body into different shapes and positions. Then try bending, turning, and lifting your child's body. Next, it is your child's turn to be the sculptor. Stand, sit, or lie while he shapes your body. Offer no resistance and hold each new position still until your child moves it again.

poem dance

Directions

Choose a favorite poem and read it aloud. Select a few of the ideas, words, or images in the poem and express them in movement with your child. Some ideas will suggest how to move and others will suggest a mood, feeling, or environment. Some poems can be read and moved to for their rhythmic quality. Have one person read the poem while the other moves to the rhythm of the words.

Dancing to the poem will make that poem become more alive and meaningful as well as being a memorization tool. Try singing the words with the melody from a favorite song, or freezing while the words are being read and dancing in a quiet space after the sentence.

A Light in the Attic by Shel Silverstein has wonderful descriptive poems about cows and other animals, clowns, facial expressions, movements like shaking, skipping, dancing, and tickling.

playing with dance

Directions
Get everyone involved in this group dance. Put on some lively music that everyone likes and clear a big open space. Someone start as the leader by making up some interesting, funny steps that everyone can follow along with for a few minutes. When the leader raps someone else on the shoulder, everyone begins to follow along with the new leader's steps for a few minutes before the next leader is tapped. Keep going as long as you like.

chiffon dancing

Directions

Provide yourself and your child with chiffon scarves. Throw them into the air and watch them float down to the ground. After each scarf has settled, imitate the scarf movements in the air and down to the ground with your own movements. Try this several times. Drape the scarf over your head or shoulders and dance. Think of other ways that you and your child can dance with the scarves: making large circles and zigzags, leaping over them, wrapping up, and then unwinding.

spaghetti dance

Directions

Lie down on the floor with your child very stiff and straight. Imagine you are uncooked spaghetti and roll over and over. Now imagine you are being put into hot water to cook. Feel your bodies getting softer and softer. When the water boils, make your bodies swirl and twist just as spaghetti would. Finally, imagine you have been drained and tossed with butter or sauce. What movements would result? This is a fun dance to do on a night you're cooking spaghetti so your child can see how the spaghetti starts out, and how it does dance and swirl in the water.

growing and shrinking

Directions
Stand where you have lots of room. Imagine you and your child are each in a giant bubble. Reach out and try to touch the walls of the bubble. Imagine the bubble begins to get smaller and smaller until you can squeeze it up and hold it tightly in your hand. Now let it go and feel it expand all around you again. As the bubble gets bigger, you and your child grow bigger too.

education

by bus, boat, or train

Directions

Kids are intrigued with all methods of transportation, from wheels on the bus to hot air balloons. Experiencing a mode of transportation that isn't part of a child's daily life is quite an experience. Select a method of transportation that you and your child don't use often. If you drive everywhere in the car, then you might choose the local bus, train, ferry, subway, or cable car. Do a little research online, or find a book in the library that has detailed picture and description of how the chosen mode of transportation works. Ask your child questions; how do you think the wheel was discovered? How does the train keep moving forward? Encourage imagination and creative explanations rather than the right answer.

Buy a round-trip ticket and go for a ride.

i see

Materials
1. Illustrated magazines

Directions
Sit with your child and turn the pages of the magazine pretending to be on a mission to find a particular object or person. For example, you might look for a mother with a baby, a child playing with a toy, an animal of any kind, or whatever your child suggests. Turn the pages until you find a picture that fits. Then make up a story about the picture. Ask your child if she likes the picture and why she likes it. Discuss the sense of sight with your child and how it has been developed in us so that we can find out about our environment and ourselves. Sight is for looking and learning.

farm visit

Directions

Depending on the time of the year, you and your child can make plans to visit a farm. For example, around Halloween and Thanksgiving there are pumpkin farms to visit. Before Christmas, there are Christmas tree farms. At other times of the year, there are vegetable farms, orchards, daily farms, flower farms, and sheep or goat farms. Use the telephone to make arrangements and don't forget to dress appropriately. Do a little research online or get a book from the library so you can read about the workings of the farm. Make a list of questions your child might want to ask the farm owner or employees. When visiting the farm, take pictures so you can make a picture book when you return that explains the workings of the farm.

flotation experiment

Materials

1. Bathtub or sink
2. Lightweight objects—corks, feathers, plastic lids or caps, sponges
3. Heavier objects—paper clips, pencils, buttons

Directions

Fill the bathtub or sink with water. Set all the objects nearby within your child's reach. The object of this activity is to see which objects float and which ones don't. Some may float for a while and then sink. Some small objects may sink immediately, while some large objects stay floating. Make a guessing game out of it. Before putting the item in the sink, guess if it will sink or float. Ask your child questions: Why do you think this object is sinking? What makes this float? Then notice if the water goes up on the side of the sink when an object is added. Let your child hold each object in his hand, determining if it is heavy or light. Have him hold one object in each hand and say which is heavier.

muddied waters

Materials
1. 3 clean jars
2. Garden soil
3. Sand
4. Dirt
5. Stick

Directions
The object of this activity is to observe how water gets muddy and clears again. Fill the jars two-thirds full of water. Drop a handful of garden soil in one, a handful of sand in another, and a handful of dirt in the third jar. Watch how the soil, sand, and dirt settle. Stir each jar with a stick. Notice how the water changes color and that each jar is a slightly different color. Now wait and let the jars settle again. Discuss what you and your child observed.

bear hospital

Materials
1. Old sheeting
2. Masking tape
3. Band-Aids
4. Scissors

Directions
Tear narrow strips of old sheeting to make bandages. Cut out triangular shapes too. Show your child how to make an arm sling and how to tape down bandages. Using her bears, dolls, and stuffed toys as patients, have your child pretend that she is in a hospital or clinic where the toys must be treated and repaired. Be careful to handle the toys gently.

who's hiding?

Materials
1. Pictures of animals and favorite things
2. Cardboard
3. Glue and scissors
4. Felt markers

Directions
Cut out the pictures of people, animals, and favorite things. Paste them onto squares or shapes of cardboard. On separate cards, write the names of each picture that you've glued to a card: dog, apple, house, duck. The object of the activity is to teach your child to match the word cards with the picture cards. It is often easier for children to remember words when they are looking at and naming familiar people, places, and things. While your child is watching, turn one picture card face-down and ask "Who's hiding under here?" Your child then tries to guess by placing the matching word card where he thinks it belongs. Once you have the idea of the game, try putting three or more picture cards down at a time.

fire station visit

Directions

Go to the library and find a book about firemen and firefighting. Read the book to your child a few times and write down the list of questions your child asks about how houses start on fire, who gets to be a fireman, and how they get to the fire so fast. Explain the responsibilities of the local firefighters and how to call them in an emergency. Call the fire station first to make arrangements and then take your child to visit. A firefighter will gladly show your child around and answer any questions. Make sure you ask to see the heavy jackets firemen wear and how they store their boots and pants all ready to jump into when the siren rings.

a morning at work

Directions.
Most mornings, children are aware that one or more adults in the family are going off to work. Make the necessary arrangements to have your child accompany or visit the adult one morning. Show your child around the workplace and explain what goes on. As a result, your child will understand better where the adults go and what they do while they are away from home.

anatomy for kids

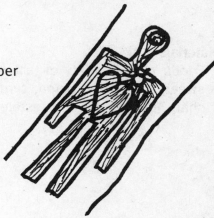

Materials
1. Butcher paper or plain newsprint paper
2. Paints, felt pens, or crayons

Directions
Trace your child's body as she lies face-down or face-up on the paper. Tape the paper in place on the floor. Have your child proceed to draw her body parts onto the outline of her body where they belong. Start with obvious parts: nose, ears, fingernails, teeth, hair, and belly button. More difficult parts might include: elbows, kneecaps, chin, and heels. For older children, you could label the inner organs: heart, lungs, kidneys, and liver.

taste and tell

Materials

1. Foods with a variety of tastes— sweet, salty, sour, bland, syrupy, sharp, bitter, rich, and tasteless

Directions

The purpose of this activity is to make your child more aware of the sense of taste. Gather a variety of foods in small amounts. If you like, your child can close her eyes while tasting each one. After each food, discuss the taste. Begin to distinguish between the main taste bud differentiation: sweet, sour, bitter and salty. Ask your child to say which are his favorite foods and why. Try combining foods of different tastes. How did the taste change when the foods were combined?

listen to the world

Directions

This activity can be done inside or outside. Sit beside your child or back-to-back, and close your eyes. Concentrate on listening to all the sounds around you. Listen to the world. Is the refrigerator humming, a plane flying overhead, the dog barking, or telephone ringing? Say what you hear. Can your child identify all the sounds? Are there any soft sounds? High sounds? Take turns being very quiet and then share what sounds you can hear.

the electric show

Materials
1. Hair comb
2. Small pieces of paper
3. Balloon

Directions
To create a static electricity field, have your child run a comb through his hair a few times. Then experiment by picking up pieces of paper with the comb. Next, blow up the balloon and tie it. Rub the balloon a couple of times against your child's arm or leg. Next, put the balloon against the wall and note how it sticks there. Go online and find out about static electricity so that you can explain how and why it works to your child.

heads and faces collage

Materials
1. Old magazines
2. Plain paper
3. Glue
4. Scissors
5. Crayons or felt pens

Directions

Go through the old magazines with your child and find pictures of heads, faces, hair, glasses, earrings, and hair pieces—anything having to do with the head. Cut them out, then glue them onto a sheet of plain paper to form a collage. If parts of the faces or heads are missing, have your child draw the missing parts with crayons or felt pens. As you work, identify and name everything.

backwards day

Directions

Today you are going to turn your child's day around! Everything that usually happens at the start of the day will take place in the evening, and vice versa. Begin the day with a bedtime story and a bath, take the afternoon nap in the morning, and have breakfast at night. Think of other things that you could do in keeping with a "backwards" day. Do not forget to let your child know what's going on and ask her for ideas.

tweezers and tongs

Materials
1. Tweezers
2. Kitchen tongs
3. Variety of small and very small objects
4. Empty egg cartons

Directions
Select various objects that require children to use tongs or tweezers to pick them up. Examples are: cereal, cut-up raw vegetables, cooked rice, dried fruits, corks, sugar cubes, cotton balls, buttons, and cooked peas. Experiment with how to grasp, squeeze, and move the object from one egg carton to the other. Once your child gets good at tweezing and dropping, have a race, or count how many objects can be moved before one is dropped.

color grouping

Directions
Ask your child to look at the things in his room, around the house, and outside and group them by the different colors. Which things are red, white, or green? Look to see how many shades of the same color you can locate. Ask your child what his favorite color is. Also ask which he thinks look good together. Finally, ask which colors are "warm" colors (reds, oranges, yellows) and which colors are "cold" (blues, greens, purples). It is also fun to carry around paint samples trying to match the color of the sample to various things in the home and outside. Cards of paint samples are available at most hardware and home supply stores.

evaporation experiment

Materials
1. 2 clear plastic cups
2. Felt marker
3. Clear plastic wrap
4. Water

Directions
Partly fill the plastic cups with water so that they both have the same level of water. Mark the levels with the marker. Seal one of the cups with plastic wrap. Leave it for a day. Look at both cups and mark where the water levels are. Do this for a few more days, marking the levels each day and noting any change. Your child will notice that the water level goes down in the cup that has no cover. Where does the water go? Talk about the water disappearing and explain what evaporation is.

steamy experiment

Materials
1. Teakettle
2. Metal saucepan lid
3. Water

Directions
Boil water in the teakettle, being careful that your child does not touch the kettle or the steam as it comes out. Turn the heat to low when the water boils. As the steam comes out of the spout, hold the saucepan lid in front of it. Point out how the steam turns into water once it touches the lid. Recount how the water in the kettle turns into steam and then turns back into water again. Find other examples of condensation for your child to notice, such as drops of water on the bathroom window or breath on a cold glass.

energy from the sun

Materials
1. 3 used cans with the labels removed
2. White water-based paint
3. Black water-based paint
4. Brushes
5. Thermometer

Directions
Paint the outside of two of the cans—one with white paint, one with black paint. Fill each can with the same amount of water (use a measuring cup) from the faucet. Place the cans on a sunny window ledge or in the sun somewhere. Let them sit for about three hours. Now take the temperature of the water in each can. Which can has the warmest water? Why was this so? Explain to your child the principle of solar energy and its benefits.

babies collage

Materials
1. Old magazines such as *Parenting*, *Child*, *Working Mother*, or *Parents*
2. Scissors
3. Glue or paste
4. Old book, notebook, or piece of cardboard

Directions
This activity is ideal for children who are expecting a baby sister or brother. Go through some old magazines with your child and find pictures of babies and the things that babies need, such as diapers, bedding, toys, or clothes. Cut them out and then you and your child can arrange them on the pages of a book (gluing a piece of white or colored picture over the story), in a notebook, or on the piece of cardboard like a collage. Have your child make up a story about what life might be like with a new baby. Write the story underneath the pictures.

feely box

Materials
1. Large cloth bag or pillowcase
2. Assortment of toy animals and familiar objects
3. Rubber band

Directions
Without your child watching, choose three or four toys or objects that belong to her (for example, a hairbrush, teddy bear, shoe, or toy truck). Place one object in the bag and tie the open end with the rubber band. Ask your child to guess what the object is by feeling the outside of the bag. Remove the object when the guess is successful and continue until there are no objects left. Have your child search the house for objects while you close your eyes and then have a chance to feel and guess.

fun sign language

Directions
Involve your child in making up signals with their hands, arms, and fingers. Each signal should stand for a word or expression. Keep it simple and see how many your child can come up with and remember. This could become a game—a secret or private language between you and your child.

transportation collage

Materials
1. Old magazines
2. Scissors
3. Glue or paste
4. Cardboard
5. Black felt pen

Directions
Sit with your child and go through old magazines looking for pictures of cars, boats, planes, and other means of travel. Also look for pictures that show the inside of these vehicles. Cut them out and have your child arrange them on the sheet of cardboard. Glue or paste them to form a collage. When the glue dries, label some of the pictures with a black felt pen. When a parent has to travel somewhere, use the collage to show kids exactly what form of transportation the parent will be using.

long distance sounds

Materials
1. 2 paper cups
2. Long piece of string

Directions

This is how to make a simple long distance telephone. Pierce a small hole in the bottom of each paper cup. Thread the string through each hole and tie a knot so that the cups are connected. Now each of you take a cup and stand apart from each other, keeping the string taut. One talks into the cup while the other puts the cup to his ear. If words are too difficult to understand, just make different sounds.

my own scales

Materials
1. Wire coat hanger
2. 2 strong paper plates
3. 4 pieces of string, 30" long

Directions
Make four small holes in the edges of each paper plate. Using two lengths of string per plate, thread them through the holes to make a cross on the back of the plates. Hang plates from each corner of the hanger. Hang the coat hanger from a doorknob. Find some small stones or marbles and place them on one of the plates. Now find other things that will balance the other plate. Try other balances to see which is heavier: a cookie or a bunch of grapes, a toy car or a sock, a bar of soap or an orange.

what fits in this jar?

Materials

1. Jars of different sizes with different
   size openings

Directions

Line the jars up on the counter. Hunt around the house for objects of various sizes. Ask your child to look at the object and guess before trying which jars the object might fit into. Talk about the size of the object compared to the opening of the jar. Help her think of things that are not normally found in jars and see if they would fit. After your child guesses, let her try to fit the object into the jar. If it doesn't fit, try another guess.

fill in the rainbow

Materials
1. Colorful fabric
2. Old magazines
3. Scissors
4. Pencils
5. Large sheet of paper
6. Glue

Directions
Draw the outline of a rainbow onto the paper. Show your child which color goes in which area of the rainbow by pasting on a scrap of fabric or a piece of colored paper. Explain to your child to only glue on the same color in each separate ring. Go through the fabric and magazines to find the different colors. This project could take several sessions and might be a good one for other members of the family to help with.

environment

recycled mail

Materials
1. Used envelopes—any shape
2. Glue stick

Directions
Collect used envelopes. Ask parents to carefully open their mail so as not to tear envelopes. Glue down the flaps and wait until dry. Now use the backs of the envelopes for scratch paper, lists, painting, drawing, and construction projects. Stamps can be soaked off before gluing and saved for sticker projects or for a stamp collection. Think of other ways to use the recycled envelopes, especially ones with clear windows in them.

natty napkin rings

Materials
1. Heavy cardboard tube
2. Water-based paints
3. Crayons
4. Felt pen

Directions
Encourage your family to use cloth napkins at mealtimes. If everyone in the family has his or her own napkin ring, napkins can be used over again and your family will save on water and laundry soap.

To make individual napkin rings, decorate the outside of the cardboard tube with paints, crayons, or a colorful collage. When completely dry, an adult can slice the tube into one-inch sections with a sharp knife. Smooth the edges with an emery board. Put each family member's name on the outside of one of the rings. When ready to use, pull a napkin through the ring starting with a corner.

bottle bins

Materials
1. 2 sturdy boxes
2. Colored paper and magazine pages
3. White paper (recycled) or paint
4. Water-based felt pens
5. Paste or glue

Directions
Sort and store glass containers in your home. Decorate the outside of one box with colored paper and pens and the other with white paper or paint. Find a place to keep the boxes, such as in the garage. Start collecting empty glass bottles and jars. Remove the caps and lids and rinse the dirty ones. Place glass bottles and jars in the white box and newspaper in the colored box. Most communities pick up recycling when they pick up the trash each week. Make sure you know how they expect it to be divided so that yours won't be left on the curb.

popcorn packaging

Materials

1. Popcorn—unsalted and unbuttered

Directions

Popcorn is a safe, inexpensive, and lightweight material to use in packaging. The next time you or your child have to send a precious parcel somewhere, pack it in popcorn instead of paper or Styrofoam. Popcorn can also be used when storing or moving glassware, plates, and other breakables. Prepare as much popcorn as you think you will need, allow it to cool, and store in an airtight container until ready for use.

recycling center roundup

Directions

Most families have a recycling bin and schools talk about the importance of putting bottles and cans in separate trash cans so they can be used again in an attempt to preserve our environment. Take your child to a recycling center or local trash site where they can view how trash is dumped, how the yard waste is set aside to be used in landfills, and where the items that can be reused are placed. Kids love to watch the large machinery moving piles of trash. It's fun to point out how much people throw away. Raise the question of where all the trash goes. Point out how recycling reduces the amount of trash we generate.

kid's kompost

Materials
1. Wooden box
2. Lawn clippings and leaves
3. Vegetable peelings

Directions
Gardens, whether they are in pots or in the open ground, need soil conditioner and extra nutrients. Here is how to make your own compost. Place a bottomless wooden box directly on the dirt, in the shade. Whenever the lawn is mowed save some of the grass clippings and spread them in the box. Alternate the clippings with layers of leaves, vegetable peelings, and other clean organic garbage. Turn over the compost occasionally and soon you will have a rich soil supplement to use in the garden or in the horticulture projects listed in this book.

rag bag

Materials
1. Used clothes
2. Old towels and washcloths
3. Worn-out cloth diapers
4. Old socks

Directions
Instead of throwing old clothes away, cut or tear them into good size pieces for use as rags. Cotton T-shirts and old cloth diapers are best. Old socks are good for dusting and cleaning jobs. Your child can put his hand inside and help with the housework. Place the rags and socks in a specially marked bag for use in cleaning jobs and art projects. Make sure the bag is placed or hung low enough for children to reach.

earth beautification

Materials
1. Garbage bag

Directions
Beaches, parks, and roadways can quickly become spoiled by litter. On your next outing to the beach, park, or walk around town, take along a garbage bag, preferably a burlap sack. As you walk, pick up all the garbage that is lying on the ground and drop it into the sack. At the end of your "Earth beautification" walk, empty the sack into a garbage bin. Save the sack for your next cleanup effort.

angel bird feeders

Materials
1. Snowy day
2. Bird food—corn kernels, seed, fruits

Directions
Make an angel in the snow by lying on top of a flat patch of snow and moving your arms and legs back and forth. Get up without making footprints in the angel. Use corn kernels, seeds, wild bird seed, cranberries, or other food birds will eat to make a design within the angel, sprinkling the food here and there. Sit back and watch the birds enjoy your creation.

bug treats

Materials

1. Apple cores

Directions

Bugs are tiny, but they play a very important role in keeping the Earth healthy. Protecting and feeding them is beneficial to everyone. Bugs should be moved to safety if they are on a sidewalk or playing area. Bugs like to eat organic garbage. Save your apple cores and place them in the garden or in corners of the yard. Soon the apple core will disappear. Bugs often feed at night, so have your child check every day to see how much of the apple core is left.

slug trap

Materials:
1. Cottage cheese container and lid
2. Scissors
3. Stale or inexpensive beer

Directions:
Cut three or four openings in the rim of the cottage cheese container. In the garden where the slugs are usually found, dig a hole large enough to fit the container, leaving it an inch above the soil level. Partially fill the container with beer, seal with the lid, and lower into the hole, packing the soil around it. Slugs come out at night to feed on garden plants and will be attracted to the aroma of the beer. Check each morning for dead slugs (which can be added to a compost heap) and replace with more beer weekly.

snip snap

Materials
1. 6-pack rings
2. Scissors

Directions
Plastic six-pack rings often wind up in the ocean and can kill sea birds and fish when their heads get caught in the rings. When your child finds a six-pack ring, show him how to use the scissors to snip the plastic into small sections. Put the sections in the garbage or in a plastic recycling bin.

paper press

Materials
1. Newspaper
2. Blender
3. 12 x 8 inch piece of screening
4. 13 x 9 inch tray
5. Small wooden board

Directions
Make your own paper. Tear three pages of a newspaper into small pieces. Drop pieces into a blender and add five cups of water. Blend until paper is turned into pulp. Pour the pulp onto the screen in the tray to drain, spreading pulp evenly. Lift out the screen and place it inside several sheets of dry newspaper. Flip over the newspaper so that screen is on top of the pulp. Press out the excess water with the board. Open the newspaper and remove the screen. Leave the newspaper and let the pulp dry. When dry, carefully peel the new paper off the newspaper. It can now be used to write or draw on.

the tree of life

Materials

1. A large tree with many branches

Directions

Children see trees almost every day. Trees can be used to remind children of the connectedness of all life, and of human beings in particular. Have your child look closely at each branch, tracing where it attaches to the trunk and where it leads to. Imagine one little twig is your family. The branch would be your neighborhood, and a larger branch, your town. All the branches connect to form your country and the whole tree represents all the countries in the world. Notice how we all have the same trunk and roots. Point out how we all need each other in order to make a beautiful and healthy tree.

zoo project

Directions
Your child can help save and protect endangered animals. Call the local children's zoo or nature reserve. Ask if it has an "animal adoption" program. If so, let your child choose an animal, preferably an endangered species, and see how much she can learn about it. Perhaps there will be some things she can do for the animal or ways your child can help the zoo save more animals from extinction.

family

bedtime ritual

Directions

Bedtime can be a magical time for you and your child if you take the time to create a bedtime ritual. This ritual sets the tone each night, and gives your child a schedule to follow and something to look forward to before falling asleep. Begin the ritual about an hour before planned bedtime. Here is an example: bath for twenty minutes with at least half of that time for playing, read stories for another twenty minutes, spend five minutes together talking about the good things that happened that day, and then take a few minutes for a prayer, meditation, thought, or remembrance, which can be sung or spoken softly.

DAD

lighter thoughts

Directions

This is a relaxing, stress-relief activity that can be done as part of a bedtime ritual or at other times during the day to help you and your child unwind. Lie down and close your eyes. Talk softly to your child. Make up an imaginary place and describe it. Maybe you are lying under a tree, or on the beach, or in the middle of a soft, cloudlike pillow. Take a deep breath in and imagine you are breathing in the warmth and the silence. Breathe out anything sad or upsetting that might have happened that day. If you know of a problem your child has encountered, say it out loud as you are breathing out. When you breathe in, think of happy, light thoughts; mention something fun you like to do together, a favorite food, or good memory. Continue breathing in the good thoughts and out the bad ones for at least five minutes. Encourage your child to say the good and bad thoughts while you breathe in and out.

earth's small treasures

Materials
1. Egg carton
2. Glue
3. Photo of child and
   other family members

Directions
Go on a hike or stroll with your child. As you walk, explain the wonders and miracles of nature: how big trees start from tiny seeds, how rocks are formed, and how flowers produce colored petals. Collect some of these "treasures" and when you get home glue them into the recesses of an egg carton. Look through books or magazines to find pictures of baby and adult animals. Glue a photo of your child, family members, and animals into the egg carton recesses and talk about how all living things are part of nature's treasure.

family ties

Materials
1. Pictures from magazines depicting families
2. Family photos
3. Pictures of grandparents and babies

Directions
The object of this activity is to spend time with your child talking about what it means to be a family. Use the pictures to point out why families love and support each other and how important children are to every family. Show the pictures and photos to your child and encourage questions and comments. Discuss new babies, brothers and sisters, grandparents, single parents, and other relevant topics. Point out that families come in all different shapes and sizes and that you don't have to be born into a family to be part of it. Accept your child's opinions and ideas and reinforce her feelings of belonging to your family.

nurse duty

Directions

Moms and dads are expected to care for the sick children in the house. Why not teach children how to care as well? When a member of your family is sick, make up a "nurse duty" schedule. This schedule would give each family member certain hours each day to be responsible for making sure the sick person is cared for, has water to drink, something to read, someone to talk to if they want to talk, food, enough blankets, and help getting around. Emphasize to the children how good it feels to be cared for when not feeling well. When the child is sick, they can expect the same treatment from other family members. Children of all ages love to feel needed, and often they care very much but don't know what to do to help; this will give them something they can do to show how much they care.

stick puppets

tiny tots Puppet Show

Materials
1. Old magazines
2. Extra family photos
3. Construction paper or cardboard
4. Lengths of thin dowel, popsicle sticks, bamboo, or garden stakes
5. Wood glue

Directions
Find pictures of people who are important to your child: family members, baby-sitter, teacher, friend, or themselves. Cut out the person and paste each one onto the construction paper or cardboard. Let it dry. Glue the person to the sticks near the top. Tell stories with the puppets about the real people they represent. The interactions can be realistic or imaginary, but encourage your child to have and present his own ideas.

taped esteem

Directions

Children believe what they hear about themselves. Make a cassette tape or CD to give to your child, including the most positive things you can say about her. While making the recording, look at one of your fondest pictures of the child. With love and enthusiasm, say things like, "I really like it when you...I appreciate the way you...It always makes me smile when you...I think it's wonderful that you...I'm glad that you...You are a special person because..." Whether the child listens to it while falling asleep or at a time of difficulty, the taped reassurances will affect her mood. It really is true that we become what we believe about ourselves.

mood swings

Directions

Sit across from your child and explain that you are going to make some faces that tell what mood you are in. Make a variety of faces—happy, sad, worried, surprised, mad, tired, shy, or bored. Hold a book or sheet of paper in front of your face between changes. Now have your child make faces and you guess the mood. Take turns experimenting with facial expression. This is a good way to help your child recognize emotions.

chore chart

Materials
1. Piece of paper
2. Markers

Days	Brian	Nicole	Jake
Monday			
Tuesday			
Wednesday			
Thursday			
Friday			

Directions
Ever notice the help wanted signs hanging on bulletin boards around town? Here's your chance to get the extra help you need around the house without nagging. Make up a sign writing what you need help with. Cut tabs at the bottom for the kids to rip off and bring to you. You might write that you need someone to clean the trash out of your car, then on the tab write how much you will pay for ten minutes of work, fifteen minutes of work, and so on. If your child wants the job, he brings you the tab.

fingerprinting

Materials
1. Stamp pad (the kind that cleans up with soap and water)
2. White paper
3. Magnifying glass

Directions

Have your child make a set of her own fingerprints on the white paper using the stamp pad. Start with the thumb, rolling from one side to the other to make a clear print. Add each fingertip. Wash hands. Make thumb- and fingerprints of other members of the family, making sure to put a name with each set of prints. Examine the prints with a magnifying glass and talk about the fact that fingerprints are unique to each person. Talk about how special each person in your family is, and how wonderful it is that we are all so different with unique talents and traits.

dream file

Directions

Dreaming is one of the great motivators in life. Set out a pile of old magazines and let everyone cut out pictures that represent the dreams they have for their lives. Maybe they want to ride a horse, fly an airplane, or own a harp. Each person can glue the cutout pictures onto a piece of colored paper or make a collage. Be sure to include your name and the date before placing the pictures into a file. Keep this file in a special place and encourage everyone to add to it now and then. Have fun and give your imaginations free rein. Take the dream file out from time to time to check which dreams have come true.

family time capsule

Materials

1. Strong, sealable container
2. Family mementos
3. Daily newspaper
4. Photos of the family

Directions

Fill the container with a collection of family items that represent each member of the family. Have your child choose what he considers important or valuable. Put everything in the container and add the day's newspaper and photos of everyone. Seal the container and attach a note to the outside saying when the container is to be opened—one year, three years, five years, or ten years away. Finally, put the container in a safe place.

family contests

Directions

It's fun to play together as a family. Here are some fun competitions that everyone can participate in.

- **Balance contest**: Each person stands on one foot, holding a piece of the string in her hand. On the count of three, each challenger tries to unbalance her opponent by pulling on the string; the loser is the first person to put a foot down.
- **The longest apple peel**: You'll need an apple for each person and a vegetable peeler. Each person gets a chance to peel an apple. When everyone is done, measure who has the longest unbroken peel—then make an apple pie for dessert!
- **Coin spinning**: Make sure to give everyone a few practice spins, then see who can spin a coin the longest. Use a timer or have the same person count for each contestant (the counter could count faster for the younger kids to make it fair).
- **Laughathon**: Try to make opponents laugh by cracking jokes and making faces, the first person to laugh is the loser.
- **Hula hoop**: See who can keep the hula hoop going for the longest amount of time.

Think of other silly competitions you can add to this list!

i remember game

Directions
Because we are unique individuals, we all remember things differently. We may be in the same place at the same time, but each one will have different memories of a particular event. Have each person pick out a few photos from a recent past event that everyone in the family was present for. Someone start by telling the story in great detail from his point of view. After a few minutes, the next person gets to tell her version. Isn't it fun to see how different people interpret different events? Make sure everyone can see the humor in the varied versions rather than interrupting or telling the person they are wrong. In fact, there is only one rule to this game—everyone is right!

most responsible thing to do

Directions

Get some 4" x 6" cards, and write each of the following situations on a card:

I forgot to take my lunch.

I lost my house key.

The toilet overflows.

I get home and no one is there.

I fall and cut myself.

I need a ride and someone I don't know offers to take me.

A friend does something bad and I know about it.

I break mom's favorite vase when she's not home.

I owe a friend money but don't have any to pay it back.

It's a family occasion but I want to go out with a friend.

My sister/brother lends me a sweater and it gets torn.

The house next door is burning and the fire truck arrives.

I hear my mom say something on the phone that worries me.

You can make up some of your own too.

To play the game, put all cards face down in the middle of the table. The first person picks up a card and reads it. Everyone playing gets to think what the most responsible thing to do would be in that situation. The person with the card gets to call on each person and listen to each opinion. After all the opinions have been given, using bits and pieces of any of the opinions offered, the cardholder announces his version of the most responsible action. In the same way, the cardholder listens to all opinions about what the least responsible thing to do would be. Each person gets to be cardholder until all the cards are gone.

question scavenger hunt

Directions

Make a list of five to ten questions to give to each of the children who will be present for a big family dinner where relatives, friends, or neighbors might be invited. Tell the kids they are going on a scavenger hunt to find the answers to the questions you've given them. They get the answers by asking the grownups the questions.

Some question ideas: Who was mom's first grade teacher? Where did dad go to grade school? What was the first name of grandma's first date? Make up fun questions that the kids would not know the answer to. The person who finds all their answers first is the winner. Pair younger kids up with older kids or tell them the question they are supposed to ask and then write down the answer for them.

i believe wallpaper

Materials
1. Drawing paper no bigger than 8" x 11"
2. Crayons or markers
3. Scissors
4. Tape

Directions
This is an ongoing activity that can be used to decorate your child's bedroom. Start by asking your child to draw pictures of people, places, beliefs, objects, and dreams that are important things in his life. One day he might draw himself, the next a favorite spot in the garden. Attach the pictures to the bedroom wall where a border would be appropriate; near the ceiling is a possibility. Add to the border as your child completes each drawing. If the entire family wants to participate, pick a room in the house that everyone shares and hang the pictures as a temporary border in that room.

people are good

Directions

This activity is an opportunity to talk with your child about the good-ness all people have inside them. Ask your child to suggest some ways to be kind to others and to respect all people regardless of how they look, talk, or live. It is important to build your child's trust and toler-ance. Make a game of imagining what another person's life is like: someone who is handicapped, a homeless or sick person. If possible, observe people when you are out, pointing out someone different from yourself. Talk about the goodness that person has inside her, the fun things she might like to do, and how your child might try to recognize the good in others.

feel-good notebook

Materials

1. Small notebook for each person in the family

Directions

Each night after dinner or before bedtime, have everyone write in their notebooks one to six things that happened that day that made them feel good. For younger kids who cannot yet write, have them tell an adult who will write and date the entry for them. The idea is to focus on the positive experiences that each day brings. Too often the bad or worrisome events are remembered and talked about, while the simple smile, the fun game at recess, a lunch with a new friend, or the laughter of a good joke goes unnoticed. Have everyone share what they've written.

silly sentence play

Directions

If your family is dramatic, here's a fun one for you. First, on index cards, write down ten sentences like the following:

Look, a cat climbed through the window!
I have to go to the farm.
Can you believe what Allen did?
That was the day of the earthquake.

Next, decide on a scene to act out, like going to the zoo, riding horses, playing at a park, or attending a birthday party. Place all the sentence cards face down on the floor where you will be acting out the scene. Begin acting out the play, and whenever someone feels like it, they can pick up a card and read what it says. The sentences always sound funny because they are completely off the subject! Make up more sentences and keep playing.

postcard memories

Directions

Wherever you go these days, you can find a postcard with a picture of that place on it. Make it a family tradition to buy a postcard at every spot you visit. Each time you buy one, somebody writes a little note on the back. Include the date, special memories or events, and the names and ages of all the travelers present. Mail the postcards home to yourselves and collect them in a special box. Whenever anyone wants to, you can play "pick a postcard." Whatever card you pick, tell your story about what's pictured on the postcard.

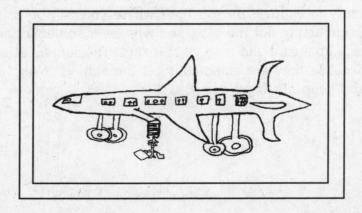

box breakfast

Materials
1. Small boxes of cereal
2. Fresh fruit
3. Picnic foods and drinks
4. Boxes (e.g., shoe boxes)

Directions
This is an activity for a parent and child to do together on a weekend morning to surprise the rest of the family. Prepare a boxed breakfast for each member of the family the night before. The next morning, get up early and hide the breakfasts outside. Leave clues as to the whereabouts of their breakfasts at the table where they would normally sit. While they search for the boxes, set up a picnic table and enjoy a surprise picnic breakfast together.

pin the blame on the donkey

Directions

Here's a game the whole family can play to have fun getting over pinning the blame on other people. Buy a donkey party game or simply draw a donkey and hang it on the wall. Each person gets a tail that represents the situation or person they feel like blaming for something. Everyone gets blindfolded (one at a time) and spun around three times; then, they try to pin the blame on the donkey. If the kids don't know what blame sounds like, remind them: I didn't do it—she did, it was my teacher's fault for not giving me the page number, you never told me to do it, if you were on time I would have won, he lost it, she ate it, etc. Use this game as a humorous way to point out how much blame actually takes place. After playing this game once, whenever you hear someone blaming someone else in the family, just say "hee haw."

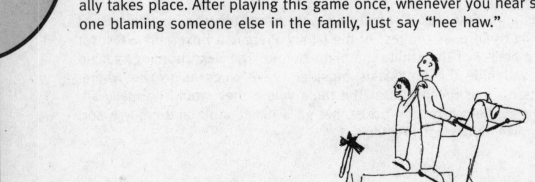

food

mashed potato sculptures

Ingredients
1. Instant mashed potatoes
2. Two eggs
3. Grated cheese (optional)
4. Baking dish
5. Pastry brush
6. Modeling tools

Directions
Prepare the instant potatoes according to the package directions. Beat in two egg yolks. Spoon the mashed potato mixture into a buttered baking dish. Make sure to wash your hands if you plan to eat the finished sculpture. Using modeling tools such as spoons, forks, and popsicle sticks, form the potatoes into shapes—animals, faces, a robot, a building, or a car. Beat the egg whites slightly and spread them onto the sculptures with the pastry brush. Sprinkle with grated cheese. Bake in the oven at 350°F until the top is brown and shiny. Cool slightly before serving.

berry ice cubes

Ingredients
1. 14 fresh or frozen blueberries
2. 14 fresh or frozen raspberries

Directions
Fill an ice cube tray with two berries in each section. Cover with water and freeze overnight. Yield: fourteen ice cubes.

homemade ice cream

Ingredients

1. 5 cups crushed ice
2. 1 gallon-size self-sealing plastic bag
3. 3 tablespoons salt
4. 1 quart-size self-sealing plastic bag
5. ½ cup whole milk
6. 1 tablespoon sugar
7. ½ teaspoon vanilla extract

Directions

Put the ice into the large plastic bag and sprinkle with salt. Pour the milk, sugar and vanilla into the small plastic bag. Seal it well, removing as much air as possible. Place the small bag into the large ice-filled bag, making sure it is completely surrounded by ice. Seal the large bag and shake vigorously, or go outside and play catch with the bag, making sure to throw it only a few feet. After about five minutes, take the small bag from the ice, open the bag to add any additional ingredients, then knead the bag to mix it together. Spoon into bowls and eat!

Flavor Ideas: Chocolate (add one tablespoon chocolate syrup), Chocolate chip (add chopped chocolate chips), Strawberry (add two tablespoons mashed fresh strawberries or one tablespoon strawberry jam), Cookies and Cream (add crushed cookies).

pudding paint

Ingredients
1. Vanilla instant pudding
2. Plastic shelf paper
3. Food coloring
4. Small bowls
5. Mixing spoons

Directions
Mix the instant pudding according to directions. Divide it up into two or three small bowls. Add a different food color to each bowl and stir until blended. Spread out the shelf paper and proceed to use the pudding mix as your child would use finger paints. Create patterns and pictures with the different colors. When your child's hands get messy, he can lick them clean.

cereal balls

Ingredients
1. ½ cup peanut butter
2. ⅓ cup honey
3. ½ cup flaked coconut
4. 2 cups favorite cereal
5. Extras—raisins, dates, banana chips
6. Large bowls

Directions
Put the peanut butter, honey, coconut, and extras in a large bowl and mix well. Stir in half a cup of the cereal and put the rest of the cereal in another bowl. Scoop out spoonfuls of the mixture and shape into balls. Roll the balls in the extra cereal. Chill in the refrigerator before eating.

container art

Materials
1. Tall glass jar
2. Dry foodstuffs—cereal, beans, lentils, crumbs, seeds, peppercorns, rice

Directions
Layer the foodstuffs one at a time until the jar is filled. The effect you are going for is many colored straight and wavy lines. This activity can be done over a longer period of time by keeping the jar in the kitchen and adding to it whenever you have extra rice, beans, beans, or cereal. Simply open the jar and add them to the layers that have already been created. Enjoy how the contours grow as the colors change.

vegetable dip

Ingredients
1. 1 cup cottage cheese
2. 2 tablespoons grated cheddar cheese
3. 1 teaspoon dill weed or parsley
4. 1 teaspoon Worcestershire sauce
5. Salt
6. Assorted vegetables

Directions
Mix the cottage cheese, grated cheese, dill or parsley, Worcestershire sauce, and a pinch of salt in a bowl. Cut or break the raw vegetables into small pieces. Dip the vegetables into the dip and eat.

egg boats

Ingredients
1. Hard-boiled eggs
2. Mayonnaise
3. Salt and pepper
4. Stick pretzels
5. Fruit roll-up

Directions
Remove the shells from the hard-boiled eggs. Cut the egg in half lengthwise. Remove the yolk and mix with mayonnaise, salt, and pepper until smooth. Cut out two triangles for sails from the fruit roll-up and stick them together with the pretzel in the middle. Put yolk mixture back into the egg half and insert the pretzel mast. Arrange several boats on a plate. When hungry, sail one right into your mouth.

homemade child's cheese

Ingredients
1. 1 cup of milk
2. Saucepan
3. 1 lemon
4. Tea strainer or sieve
5. Cheesecloth

Directions
Pour milk into pan and cook over medium heat until it just boils. Be careful not to let it boil over. Have your child watch this part. Next, add the juice of the lemon and let the milk separate into curds and whey (you might mention the "Little Miss Muffet" nursery rhyme). Let it cool a bit before pouring the curdled milk through a strainer so that the curds are left behind. Then, empty the curds onto a piece of cheesecloth. Form a ball by squeezing and twisting all the moisture out. Chill. Spread on crackers.

salad quilt

Materials

1. Seeds for salad ingredients, e.g., radishes, lettuce varieties, peppers, spinach, carrots, and rocket
2. String
3. Tent stakes
4. Pebbles or small rocks

Directions

This activity requires a fairly large plot of garden space. Prepare the soil for planting. Mark off a square 6' x 6'. Divide the space into 9 smaller squares (2' per side) using the string. Secure the lines with the tent stakes. Place pebbles or small rocks in the center square.

Plant the seeds according to the packet directions, a different one in each square except the center one. Water frequently during the growing season and harvest when ready to make fresh salads.

baked bread sandwiches

Ingredients

1. Frozen loaf of white or wheat bread (in the frozen food section, will have to rise)
2. Flour
3. Garlic salt
4. ⅓ pound salami, thinly sliced
5. ⅓ pound ham, thinly sliced
6. ⅓ pound Swiss cheese, thinly sliced
7. ⅓ pound provolone cheese, thinly sliced (you can substitute whatever meat and cheese combination your kids like)
8. 2 egg yolks, beaten
9. 12 x 16 inch pan

Directions

Thaw bread and let it rise, covered, in a warm spot according to package directions. Punch down and knead on a floured surface. Roll the dough into a 12 x 16 inch rectangle. Sprinkle with garlic salt. Tear the meat into bite-sized pieces and layer over the bread. Tear the cheese into bite-sized pieces and layer over the meat. Starting at the long end, roll the bread up tightly in jelly roll fashion. Pinch the ends together tightly and curve the roll to form a crescent. Brush with the beaten egg yolk. Bake at 375°F for twenty-five to thirty minutes or until golden brown. Let rest a few minutes before slicing. Yield: 8 to 12 servings. This is good to take along on a picnic and cut when you get there.

crunchy marshmallow balls

Ingredients
1. 5 cups of marshmallows
2. ½ stick of butter
3. Breakfast cereal
4. Deep saucepan
5. Waxed paper

Directions
Melt marshmallows and butter over low heat, stirring until blended. Let the mixture cool and then add three or more cups of cereal. Stir until cereal is evenly distributed. Have your child wet her hands and shape handfuls of the mixture into balls. When molded, place balls on waxed paper to cool and get crispier.

popsicle parade

Ingredients
1. Popsicle or ice cream sticks
2. Muffin pan or paper cups
3. Popsicle mixture

Directions
Prepare a container of popsicle mixture. This could consist of any fruit juice, flavored yogurt, chocolate milk, soda, or Kool-Aid. Pour the mixture into a muffin pan or paper cups. Put into the freezing compartment of your refrigerator. When mixture starts to freeze, remove from the freezer and insert popsicle sticks in each cup. Return to the freezer until hard. Remove from the cup or muffin pan and eat.

yummy parfaits

Ingredients
1. Parfait glass or a tall tumbler
2. Fresh fruit
3. Whipped cream
4. Pudding mix
5. Other edibles, such as chocolate chips,
   raisins, coconut, nuts, etc.

Directions
Place all the ingredients in paper cups or piles ready to scoop into the glasses. Have your child layer the ingredients (except the whipped cream) from the bottom of the glass or tumbler to the top. Add a dollop of whipped cream on the top. Encourage your child to make a few extra for a family dessert.

squishy food painting

Ingredients
1. Large Ziploc bags
2. Ketchup
3. Mustard

Directions

Put a few tablespoons of ketchup inside a Ziploc bag. Gently squeeze out the air before sealing. Lay the bag flat and smooth the ketchup until it is spread evenly. Have your child draw over the bag with his fingers. As the ketchup is pushed to the side, a white or clear line will emerge, creating a contour drawing. Fill a bag with a few tablespoons of mustard, or mix ketchup and mustard to see what happens. You may also want to put the ketchup bag on top of the mustard bag and see what colors show through.

grandma's granola

Ingredients
1. 2½ cups oatmeal
2. ½ cup coconut
3. ½ cup almonds or nuts
4. ½ cup Grape-Nuts
5. ½ cup margarine
6. ½ cup honey or sugar
7. ½ cup raisins, dates, or cranberries

Directions
In a large bowl, mix together (with hands) oatmeal, coconut, almonds, and Grape-Nuts. Melt the honey and margarine and stir it into dry ingredients. Spread evenly on a cookie tray and bake at 300°F for twenty minutes, stirring after ten minutes to make sure all the grains get browned. Remove from the oven and fold in the raisins. Cool. Store in an airtight container or eat immediately. Makes one pound.

easy cinnamon rolls

Ingredients
1. 1 package frozen bread dough
2. 4 tablespoons butter
3. ¼ cup sugar
4. ¼ cup brown sugar
5. 2 teaspoons cinnamon
6. ½ cup raisins (optional)

Frosting
7. ½ cup powdered sugar
8. 2 tablespoons milk

Directions
Thaw dough to room temperature and let rise overnight or until doubled. Pat dough into a 8"x 12" rectangle. Spread with the melted butter. Combine the sugars and cinnamon and sprinkle over the butter. Evenly distribute the raisins over the top. Starting with the longer side, roll the dough up. Seal edges tightly. With a sharp knife, cut the roll into one-inch pieces. Place rolls flat side down on a greased cookie sheet, allowing room to spread, and then let rise in a warm place until doubled in size. (These can also be baked immediately, but will produce smaller rolls). Bake at 375°F (190°C) for twenty minutes. Remove from oven, and while still warm, drizzle with frosting or honey.

Yield: twenty-four rolls.

food sculpture

Materials

1. Cheese spread—cream cheese, sour cream, onion soup mix
2. Bowl
3. Snack foods—chips, popcorn, pretzels, crackers

Directions

Prepare the cheese spread by warming three ounces of the cream cheese until it is soft. Blend in three tablespoons of sour cream and mix in a packet of soup mix. Arrange the snacks in piles and then proceed to build a sculpture, selecting from the assortment of snacks and cementing them together with the cheese spread. The cheese doesn't add a lot of strength, so it is best to keep the sculpture low. When finished, your child can have fun eating her creation.

a "cool" cake

Ingredients
1. A plain cake
2. Vanilla or white icing
3. Food coloring
4. Corn syrup
5. Chocolate syrup
6. Spatula and spoons
7. 5 paper cups

Directions
Spread the icing over the cake as smoothly as possible. Pour two table-spoons of corn syrup into each paper cup. Next, add a different food color to each cup and add chocolate syrup to one. Drip the colors onto the cakes using spoons. Let the colors run together or mix them up and experiment with patterning. For an interesting birthday cake, wait until the guests are seated and pass the iced cake around for everyone to help frost.

orange pomander

Materials
1. 2 or 3 oranges
2. Box of whole cloves
3. Colored string

Directions
Cut the oranges in half and remove the pulp without disturbing the skin. Fit the halves back together again by placing one inside the other to make ball shapes. Secure the halves by inserting cloves through both layers of skin. Insert more cloves in the orange skins, in patterns if desired. Tie colored string around the balls so that they can be hung from a closet rod. These pomanders will give a delicate scent to your clothes for many months.

pancake art

Ingredients
1. Pancake batter
2. Frying pan
3. Butter
4. Spatula
5. Soup spoon
6. Small bowl or cup

Directions
Mix the pancake batter with milk to make it slightly thin. Pour some into a small, deep bowl or cup. Melt butter in the frying pan and when it is evenly spread, remove the frying pan to the bench. Have your child take spoonfuls of batter and drip it into the frying pan to form a design. Return the frying pan to the heat. When the design starts to turn brown, pour more batter over it. Cook until the edges are dry and flip over. The design will be embedded. Finish cooking and serve.

apple plumps

Ingredients

1. Large apples—one for each member of the family
2. Baking tray
3. Apple corer
4. Butter
5. Brown sugar
6. Fillings—raisins, dates, coconut, nuts, etc.

Directions

Remove the core from each apple with the corer and sprinkle the inside of the apple with some sugar. Set the apples in a greased baking tray. Stuff the centers of the apples with the filling, pushing down firmly. Pour a little warm water into the tray, just enough to cover the bottom. Bake for thirty to forty-five minutes at 350°F. Every now and then, baste the apples with the liquid in the tray. Remove apples from the oven and eat when cooled.

wagon train

Ingredients
1. Celery
2. Carrot
3. Toothpicks
4. Peanut butter

Directions
Wash celery and cut into two-inch lengths. Scrub carrot and cut into slices. Attach four round carrot slices to celery with toothpicks to make little wagons. Fill each wagon with peanut butter or a soft cheese. Admire, then eat, making sure to remove the toothpicks first.

ice bowl

Ingredients

1. Medium-size ball (whatever size you'd like your bowl mold to be)
2. Cooking oil
3. Deep foil pan (big enough so that the ball can sit in it, and that will fit in your freezer)
4. Pastry brush

Directions

Scrub the ball clean and then paint it with vegetable oil. Place the ball in the foil pan. Fill the pan with water to an inch from the top of the pan, covering at least one-third of the bottom of the ball. Now place the pan and the ball in the freezer compartment overnight. The next day, remove the ball and the foil pan and your child will have an ice bowl in which to put ice cream or a frozen dessert. Bowl can be reused by rinsing and returning to the freezer. You can also add food color to the ball or make with a fruit juice and use it for a special event fruit salad or ice cream dish.

surprise salad

Ingredients
1. Raw vegetables
2. Slivered almonds
3. Large packet of lemon gelatin
4. 1 cup cottage cheese
5. ½ cup mayonnaise
6. Large, deep glass cake pan

Directions
Cut vegetables up into small pieces—strips, cubes, florets, wedges. Arrange them in a pattern on the bottom of the cake pan. In a bowl, dissolve the gelatin in 1-½ cups of boiling water and add 1 cup of cold water. Carefully spoon the gelatin over the vegetables. Put the cake pan in the refrigerator. Meanwhile, beat the cottage cheese and mayonnaise into the remaining gelatin. When the vegetable gelatin is firm, spread the other mixture over the top. Chill and eat.

two-tone etched cookie

Ingredients
1. Graham crackers
2. 2 oz. dark chocolate
3. Marshmallow topping
4. 1 tablespoon butter
5. Double boiler
6. Knife, brush, skewer

Directions
Melt the chocolate and butter in the top of a double boiler until smooth. Spread the graham crackers with the marshmallow topping. Dip the brush into the chocolate and paint over the marshmallow. Refrigerate the crackers for about thirty minutes. Take the skewer (or a clean nail) and scratch the chocolate layer to expose the white layer beneath. Etch different designs on each cracker. Share and eat.

edible jewelry

Ingredients
1. Lifesavers candy
2. Cheerios or Fruit Loops
3. Miniature marshmallows
4. Thread
5. Darning needle (plastic with rounded tip)

Directions
Begin by threading the needle with yarn or thread. Now see if your child can make an interesting necklace or bracelet by threading a variety of foodstuffs together. When your child is finished, she can wear and then eat the results.

ice cream cone cakes

Ingredients
1. Ice cream cones—flat-bottomed
2. Cake mix
3. Frosting mix
4. Cake decorations
5. Muffin pan

Directions
Prepare the cake mix according to directions. Spoon the batter into the cones until they are two-thirds full. Place the cones in the muffin pan and bake according to the package directions. When the cakes are cool, frost and decorate them.

tic-tac-toe

Ingredients
1. Twisted licorice
2. Two kinds of gummy-type candy
   (bears, hearts, insects)
3. Paper plate

Directions
Put the licorice on the plate creating a tic-tac-toe grid (two pieces of licorice one way and two crossing them). Each player picks what candy will represent his mark on the board. The object is for a player to get a row, across or diagonally. Take turns placing your candy on the board. Eat your candy after each game and begin again.

collage melt

Ingredients
1. Sliced cold cuts
2. Cheese slices
3. Bread
4. Scissors and knife

Directions
Butter the slices of bread and place them face down on a cookie sheet.
Use scissors to cut the meat and cheese into small shapes. Have your
child decorate each bread slice making colorful collages. Put the cookie
tray under the broiler for a few minutes until the cheese melts and the
shapes all run together. Cool and eat.

ice cream snowballs

Ingredients
1. 3 cups flaked coconut
2. ½ gallon vanilla ice cream

Directions
Line a cookie tray with waxed paper. Using an ice cream scoop, make ice cream into sixteen separate balls. Place on cookie tray and freeze until firm. Put coconut into a bowl. Remove ice cream balls from the freezer and roll each one in the coconut until completely covered. Return them to the freezer until ready to eat.

Yield: eight to ten snowballs.

outer space cookies

Ingredients
1. Chilled cookie dough
2. Cutting tools and objects

Directions
On a floured board or table, roll out the cookie dough. Have your child cut out and shape cookies that might have come from outer space. Place the cut cookies on the greased cookie sheet. Make impressions on the cookie shapes with Legos, forks, fingers, and other textured objects. Bake for fifteen minutes at 350°F.

games

sand touching

Materials
1. Sandbox or beach

Directions

Sand offers endless possibilities for discovery. Each player digs her hands under the sand. Without poking any part of the hand above the sand, try to touch your fingers or shake hands. Next, take your hands out and bury your feet, trying to touch toes while your feet remain under the sand. If the sand is damp, design a tunnel from each end until hands and fingers meet. You might also bury prizes in the sand and then create a simple treasure map with clues to where the objects can be found. For a challenge, try sand touching with one person blindfolded so that the other has to give directions; up, down, left, right, straight ahead. Classroom "sand tables" are too shallow for these games.

wolf in the woods

Directions

At the end of the day, some of us are too tired to play. Here's a game that lets everyone rest and still have fun! Pretend the living room is a forest with one wolf and several other animals running around. One person is the wolf, everyone else pretends to be other forest animals. The other animals lie on the forest floor perfectly still with their eyes wide open. No moving is allowed except for breathing, blinking, and eye movement. You're out of the game if the wolf catches you moving in any other way. The wolf is allowed to try to get the other animals to move any way she can without touching them: by making funny faces, strange sounds, or telling them jokes. The winner gets to be the next wolf.

guess who's leading

Directions

This is a mirroring game where everyone imitates the movements of the leader. To practice for the game, the oldest family member takes the role of leader first. As the leader moves, everyone else does exactly the same movements at the same time. Sitting in a circle, the leader makes slow movements with his arms, legs, and head, and everyone else imitates the same slow movements. Let each person lead for a few minutes. This is practice.

Now the fun begins. One person, called the Investigator, leaves the room while the rest secretly decide on a leader. When the Investigator is called back, the movement game begins again. The object is for the Investigator to discover who is being the leader. Once the leader is discovered, that person becomes the next Investigator, and the game goes on.

water slide

Materials
1. Large sheet of plastic: tablecloth, thick drop cloth, or roll of roofing plastic from building supply store
2. Stones or weights
3. Garden hose
4. Liquid dish detergent

Directions
Spread the plastic sheet onto the lawn. Weight the edges down with stones or other weights. The wider and longer the plastic, the less chance someone will slide into one of the edge weights. The plastic sheet may also be stabilized by using tent pins, but make sure they are pushed all the way down into the lawn. Place the hose at one edge of the plastic or designate a person to spray the slide. Turn water on, and when the sheet is completely wet, squirt some liquid dish detergent along the slide (a little bit goes a long way). Stand at least ten feet away from the start of the slide and run, sliding down the length of the plastic. Keep the plastic wet. Every now and then, move the plastic to another part of the lawn so as not to damage the grass underneath.

flying saucers

Materials
1. Small Frisbees or plastic plates
2. Popsicle sticks
3. Felt pen

Directions

This game is best played outside with plenty of space. It can be played on the snow, grass, or cement. Throw the Frisbee or plate from a base line and see how far it will fly before touching the ground. Mark the place where it lands with a popsicle stick. Throw again and try to beat the previous record. If more than one child is playing, name or decorate the popsicle sticks, one for each child.

frogs and tadpoles

Directions

This is a friendly chasing game played in the swimming pool. The adult is the frog and the child is the tadpole. The frog must keep his eyes closed and try to find the tadpole by listening to the splashing and squealing sounds. Once caught, the tadpole can become the frog and the game starts over again. This game can be played in a paddling pool or children can hold on the edge of the pool while trying to escape the pursuing frog.

wesley says

Directions
This game is an adaptation of "Simon Says" for younger children. It can be played with one child or several. Start by saying, "Wesley says touch your toes," and demonstrate by touching your toes. Your child then copies you. After you have done this a few times with simple actions and gestures, let your child be the leader and use his own name instead of Wesley. Then, add a second action, "Wesley says touch your head and turn around." Once you have two actions down, try adding a third. Let your child make up actions for you to do. Kids enjoy being the one in charge.

shadow tag

Materials
1. Playground, park driveway, or lawn
2. Bright, sunny day

Directions
The idea of this game is to try to tag someone by stepping on her shadow. First, have your child find her shadow. By changing directions and moving around, see what happens to the shadow. Experiment with how it gets bigger and smaller. Try to chase the shadow—and lose the shadow. To play tag, whoever is "it" must try to step on another's shadow. When this happens, that child or person becomes "it." When you are sick of tag, try moving your shadows in the same direction, let them dance, hold hands, or jump in the air.

balancing seal

Directions

Have you ever wondered how a seal can balance on just one fin? This activity will teach your child about balance by challenging him to hold his body up with one or more different body parts. Begin by asking your child to stand on one foot. Then try one foot and two hands, one foot and one hand. Try out different surfaces. Is it easier to balance on a wood floor or carpet? Which body parts are easiest to balance on? Does sitting on the floor count as balancing on your bottom? Are knees easier to balance on than toes? Why?

what's missing?

Materials
1. 6 unlike objects
2. Table
3. 6 similar objects

Directions
Place the six unlike objects (such as a toy, book, fork, article of clothing, slice of bread, and a coin) on the table. While the child's back is turned, remove one of the items. Ask her which one is missing. Take away another item and ask which one is missing. Continue until all objects have been taken away. Try repeating the game with similar objects, such as six pieces of cutlery or six different toys. Work up to six different books or six dominoes.

treasure hunt

Materials
1. Blank notepaper
2. Felt pens
3. Homemade treasure: favorite fruits, small bag of old jewelry, matchbox toy

Directions
This activity has to be planned well ahead of time. All clues for finding the "treasure" are to be in picture form (either drawn or taken from magazines). Make drawings of all the places you want your child to search. For example, the TV set, the outside swing, or the mailbox. Each clue directs your child to the next clue and so on until he finds the "treasure." Creating the clues is a lot of fun. Be sure to make the drawings simple and clear. Be prepared for requests to repeat the hunt over and over again.

magpie hunt

Materials
1. Notebook
2. Felt pens

Directions
Magpies are birds which collect sundry items and hoard them. This game can be played inside or outside. Give your child a list of items that you want found and brought to you. Draw pictures of the items if necessary. Items can range from large ones, such as the Sunday comics, to small ones, such as a napkin ring or a soda cracker. Before starting the game, you might like to ask your child to give you ideas for the magpie's list. To make the game more fun, give everyone the same list and see who gathers their items first. Or, if playing with only one child, time her.

hit or miss

Materials
1. 3 glass pop bottles
2. Water squirt guns
3. 3 Ping-Pong balls

Directions
Put glass bottles on a box or table outdoors. Place a Ping-Pong ball on top of each bottle. Fill the squirt guns with water (it is best to have one squirt gun per child). Have your child stand back a yard or two from the bottles, and on a signal from you, she should try to knock off a Ping-Pong ball with water from the squirt gun. Modifications can be made to make the game more of a challenge; add more bottles, stand back a few feet, allow fewer attempts.

outdoor obstacle course

Directions

The idea is to be as imaginative as possible, creating an obstacle course that includes activities that are to be done in sequence. Be sure to structure the obstacle course activities around the age level and development of the children participating. For example:

- Start at the apple tree and do three jumping jacks.
- Run around the tree two times.
- Jump in and out of a few cardboard boxes on your way to the sandbox.
- Fill two buckets with sand and carry them to the Frisbee toss.
- Toss the Frisbee into an empty trash can.
- Hop on one foot for twenty feet, then rake a basketball (with a garden rake) through a lawn chair slalom course (lawn chairs lined up several feet apart).
- Layer a pile of dress-up clothes over what you're wearing and run toward the finish line.
- At the finish line, throw a water balloon up in the air and spin around in a circle before catching it.

Rearrange the course and play again. You may want to make this a competition, timing each person, or a team event, keeping track of the total time for the entire team.

tiptoe tease

Materials
1. Treasure items, such as fresh fruit, small toy, a book

Directions
Sit on the floor with your back to your child and your eyes closed. Have a small "treasure" or prize hidden behind your back. Your child goes to the back of the room away from you and begins to tiptoe towards you, making no sound. If you hear a sound, turn around quickly and open your eyes. If you see your child move, he goes back to the start, otherwise your child must "freeze" until you turn to the front. Continue until your child has snuck up behind you. When your child reaches you, you can reward him with the treasure.

flashlight tag

Directions

Flashlight Tag is a nighttime version of the classic Tag. It's fun for the entire family; however, kids under five may want to pair up with an adult. In this version, players spread out and try to hide from one person who is designated "it." When "it" touches or catches a player, that person becomes "it." The only difference is that in Flashlight Tag, "it" doesn't do his tagging with his hands. He does it with a flashlight. When the light shines on a participant, he's "it." However, if a player can make it to a home base before she is tagged with the light she is safe. You can also set up the game so that "it" has to catch every player before a new "it" takes over. All caught players wait at home base until everyone is caught. Small children seem to prefer this version because they like getting caught!

rolling pins

Directions
Find a grassy slope in a park and make sure there are no tree stumps or sharp objects in the ground. This could also be attempted on a snowy slope, provided the child is wrapped warmly and doesn't mind having a little snow on his face. Climb to the top and lie parallel to the slope with hands and legs stretched out and together. Gently push off and roll down the slope like a rolling pin. See how far you can go before slowing to a stop.

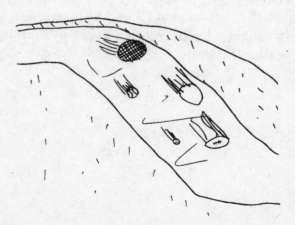

button pitch

Materials
1. Assorted buttons
2. Masking tape

Directions
Make a line on the floor with the masking tape parallel to and about six feet from a wall. Give your child and any other children ten buttons each and have them stand behind the tape facing the wall. Take turns pitching the buttons against the wall so that they fall and bounce on the floor. The goal is to have the buttons land as close to the wall as possible. To compete with another child, after each round of pitching, the child whose button is closest to the wall picks up both buttons. Keep playing until one child has all the buttons.

sprinkler games

Directions

Freeze dance: Someone stands by the sprinkler to turn it on and off. The children dance around under the sprinkler. When the water turns off everyone has to freeze. Anyone who continues to move is out. The last person left dancing gets to turn the sprinkler on and off, for the next game.

Limbo: This game challenges kids to bend low underneath the sprinkler stream of water. A hose with a spray attachment works great. To begin with, hold the hose about four feet high. The kids move underneath the water with their stomachs facing the sky. Lower the hose periodically. Players are out if any body part touches the water. In this game, the smallest usually wins!

amazing maze

Directions

Use masking tape (if you are inside) or chalk (if you are outside) and trace a room-size maze for your child to follow. Include shapes, such as triangles, squares, circles, and ovals. Instruct your child to use different steps while following the maze: skipping between the circles, leaping on the squares, or crawling on the straight lines. Include running, walking on tiptoe, hopping, and shuffling. Change the direction of the maze to include a solo dance performance whenever standing on a shape. Let your child come up with his own amazing maze trail with you following along.

turtle races

Materials
1. Cardboard
2. String
3. Crayons or markers
4. Sturdy glass tumbler

Directions
Trace a circle on the cardboard with the glass tumbler as the outline. Draw a turtle's head and legs. Add a tail. Color in both sides of the cardboard turtle, then cut it out. Make a small hole in the turtle's head and thread twelve inches of string through it. Tie the other end of the string to a table leg, about ten inches from the ground. Start with the turtle close to your fingers. Pull the string taut and watch the turtle stand. Make sure that the turtle always has his feet on the floor. Release the string and the turtle will flop forward. Keep repeating this action until the turtle reaches the table leg. Make another turtle and have a race. Try bringing the turtle backwards towards the starting point.

who remembers?

Materials
1. Photos of a family trip, birthday party, visit to the zoo, or other daily activities

Directions
In this activity, your child is encouraged to remember as much as possible about an event in her life, preferably in the right sequence. The photos are for jogging the memory. Lay the photos out on the table and see if your child can put them in order. Give plenty of hints to help the story along and paraphrase from time to time to keep the sequence on track. Use your digital camera to record one day in the life of your child, then print them up and see if she can remember the order of the day's events.

bag skit

Materials
1. Large paper bag
2. Various household items for props

This is a fun group activity, but can also be done alone and then performed for the family. Ask someone who is not playing with you to put eight to twelve props (less for younger kids) into the large paper bag. Things like a dust pan, scissors, underwear, wig, rag, card, toy, or anything else you can find. Each group of two or more is given a paper bag full of the props. The goal is to make up a skit using all the props in the bag.

newspaper sword duels

Materials

1. Newspaper
2. Masking tape

Directions

Roll up newspaper to form a long tube. Wrap masking tape around one end to form a handle. Begin the dueling game with rules for safety and good manners. The idea is to battle with the newspaper swords, not each other. Hit the tips of the swords together, backing off and circling around like a real duel. Remember to recycle the paper when the game is over.

jump the river

Materials
1. Sandbox or beach
2. Stick

Directions
Make a long, straight line with the stick. Draw another line about twenty-four inches away from the first line. Depending on the size of the child, you may want to adjust these lines by starting out closer and then making the lines wider. The lines represent the banks of the river and the idea is to jump across the river without getting wet. Take turns first stepping over the river, then hopping, and as the lines get further apart, running and jumping over the river. To make the jump more challenging, place small objects in the river or create a long, winding river so you can jump from bank to bank.

house of cards

Materials
1. Playing cards
2. Flat surface

Directions
The object of this activity is to see how many cards your child can use in constructing a house or apartment building. Lean the cards against each other forming upside-down Vs, or put two cards straight Vs up, placing one horizontally across. Start with ten cards and keep adding cards as the building gets bigger and higher. You'll have to work together. When the house ultimately collapses, count all the cards that were used. If playing with a partner, make separate houses or see what your combined efforts will produce.

who am i?

Directions
Your child is going to ask you questions that require a "yes" or "no" answer in order to find out who or what you are thinking of. Your job is to choose a person, place, or thing within your child's environment or knowledge range and keep it secret until your child has guessed correctly. He asks questions such as, is it real? Is it in my bedroom? Can I eat it?

air bowling

Materials
1. Ball
2. Net to hold ball (potato or orange sacks)
3. 9 empty quart milk cartons
4. Rope

Directions
Place the ball in the net and, using rope, suspend the ball from the branch of a tree. The ball should nearly touch the ground. Arrange the cartons in a diamond shape under the ball and to one side. The object of the game is to strike the hanging ball and see how many cartons can be knocked down. If playing with a friend, have three strikes each and see who can knock over the most milk cartons. You can also put sand, dirt, or small rocks in the bottom of the milk cartons to make them harder to knock over.

pick-up sticks

Materials
1. Wooden meat skewers
2. 2 colors of paint, plus black paint
3. Paintbrushes
4. 2 empty baby food jars

Directions
Divide the skewers in half. Put the two colored paints into the baby food jars—a different color per jar. Dip each end of half the meat skewers into one color paint and the other half into the other. Once dry, dip the other end into the same color. Dip one skewer into some black paint. To play the game, hold all the skewers in both hands upright. Let the skewers fall. The object of the game is for each player to remove his color of skewers from the pile without disturbing any other skewer (if you have more than two people, play in teams). The black one can be used to flick or poke. As long as the other sticks don't move, the player can continue to take out sticks. When the sticks move, it's the other player's turn.

indoor baseball

Materials
1. Old newspaper
2. Masking tape

Directions
Crunch some newspaper into a big ball. Start with a small ball shape and pack newspaper sheets around it. Apply masking tape to hold the ball's shape. Roll up more newspaper to form a bat shape. Find a place inside or outside the house where your child has room to run. Give your child the bat and throw the ball to her. When contact is made, your child must run to a "base" before you retrieve the ball and tag her. Be prepared to repair or replace the bats often!

horticulture

my tree and i

Materials
1. Tree seedling
2. Measuring tape
3. Camera and film
4. Scrapbook

Directions
Go to the plant nursery and buy a small, fast-growing tree—preferably have your child choose it. Plant the seedling in a special place in your garden. Take a photo of your child standing next to the tree. Measure the height of both the tree and your child and enter these measurements, together with the date and the printed photo, into the scrapbook. Every year on the tree's birthday, take another photo and more measurements. Continue entering the details into the scrapbook. Compare growth rates and changes over the years. Encourage your child to write a poem, story, or play about the tree to be included in the scrapbook. Draw pictures of the tree and other surrounding plants.

sunflower surprises

Materials
1. Packet of sunflower seeds
2. Watering can or container
3. Several 3-foot stakes

Directions

Prepare the soil in a small section of the garden or ground. Put the stakes into the ground about twelve inches apart. At the base of each stake, poke a half-inch-deep hole. Plant two or three seeds in each hole and cover with soil. Water each day. When the plants are three feet tall, tie them to the stakes with twine or narrow strips of fabric. When the backs of the flowers turn yellow, they are ready to harvest. Cut off the flowers and let them dry out for a few days. Remove the seeds and soak them in salt water for ten hours. Drain and then spread them on a cookie sheet. Bake at 200°F for an hour. Cool before eating.

edible forest

Materials

1. Packet of cress seeds
2. Packet of mustard seeds
3. Plastic plates
4. Absorbent paper, such as coffee filter or paper towel

Directions

Place several layers of the absorbent paper on the plate. Moisten it completely with water. Sprinkle some cress seeds in a single layer on one half of the plate. Cover with another dinner plate or a saucepan lid to keep the seeds in the dark. Keep the paper moist but not soggy. In three days shoots and roots will appear. Sprinkle the mustard seeds on the other half of the plate (they germinate more quickly) and replace the cover. When the seedlings are about a half-inch high, uncover them and place the plate near a sunny window. Keep moist. When the plants are green, cut with scissors and eat on sandwiches or salads.

veggie jungle

Materials
1. Fresh carrots, new potatoes, radishes
2. Shallow plastic plate
3. Small plastic animals
4. Small stones or pebbles

Directions
Select four or five vegetables with little or no foliage. Carefully cut them one to two inches from the top. Discard or cook the lower portions. Place the tops in the plate and pour in a little water. Place the plate on a sunny window ledge. In a few days, green shoots will appear. Keep water in the plate. Arrange pebbles and toy animals among the sprouting vegetables to create a jungle-like environment.

grow your own popcorn

Materials
1. 20 popcorn kernels or seeds
2. Liquid natural fertilizer

Directions
This project is done over a five-month period. Prepare the soil in a six-foot by three-foot garden spot and make two rows about eighteen inches apart. Plant ten seeds in each row about six inches and one-half inches deep. Water daily and fertilize once a month. After three months, ears of corn will appear on the plants. At four months, the tassels will be brown and the ears ready to pick. Have an adult remove the ears of corn with a knife. Pull back the husks to expose the corn. Dry in a warm place for three weeks. When bone dry, remove the kernels from the cob by scraping. Store in an airtight jar and enjoy popping your own home-grown popcorn.

sprout harvest

Materials
1. Lentils
2. Saucer
3. Coffee filter
4. Water

Directions

Place a moistened coffee filter on the saucer. Spread a layer of lentils on the paper and sprinkle on a little more water. Place the saucer on a window ledge and in two or three days they will begin to sprout. Make sure to drain the water from the saucer daily and add clean water, which will soak into the coffee filter. Harvest them in a week to eat raw, add instead of lettuce to sandwiches, or sprinkle them into salads or stir-fries.

shoots to roots

Materials
1. Dried mung beans
2. Cotton balls
3. Small bowl
4. Glass jar

Directions
Soak five mung beans (which can be bought at health food stores) in a bowl of water overnight. The next morning, drain the beans and place them on the bottom of the glass jar. Moisten several cotton balls with water and drop them over the beans. Put the jar on a window ledge. Make sure to keep the cotton balls moist, but not soggy, by adding a bit of water each day. After a few days, roots will appear and then the shoots. They will push up through the cotton balls and shape themselves in and around the cotton balls accordingly.

seedy bird's head

Materials

1. Small bird seed—about 3 tablespoons
2. Strong paper towels
3. Rubber band
4. Narrow glass jar
5. Water

Directions

Place the bird seed in the middle of the paper towel. Bring corners of the towel together and tie with the rubber band so that the bird seed is enclosed. Fill the glass jar with water. Place the ball of bird seed on top of the jar with the loose ends of paper towel pushed inside the jar and in the water like a wick. Make sure that the paper towel is kept moist so the seeds will pierce the paper and reach the light. After a few days, the seeds will begin to sprout and the ball will look like a bird with a feathered head.

leaf magic

Materials
1. Healthy begonia leaf
2. 9" square box, 5" deep or plastic container
3. Peat moss
4. Sand
5. Plastic bag

Directions
Punch holes in base of box for drainage. Fill box three inches deep with a mixture of sand and peat moss. Sprinkle with water until damp, but not soggy. Turn the leaf face down and cut through each main vein below where it starts to branch. Make a hole in the soil for the stem. Place the leaf, face-up, flat on the surface of the soil and insert the stem into the hole. Place a clear plastic bag around the box and leave somewhere cool and dry until roots start to grow. Lift the plastic and spray daily with water. Remove plastic bag and transplant begonia in a clay or plastic pot.

green bean teepee

Materials

1. 3–6 long garden stakes (at least 6')
2. 18" length of wire
3. 12–18 climbing bean seeds
   (e.g., Scarlet Runner)

Directions

Push the stakes into the garden soil to make a teepee shape, leaving an opening on the north side. Secure the upper ends with the wire and test for sturdiness. After all danger of frost has passed and when the weather has warmed, plant three bean seeds around the base of each stake. Cover the seeds with one inch of soil firmed down. Water deeply at first and then keep watered. Teepee walls fill in as the seeds grow and the result is a child's garden playhouse.

bamboo shoots

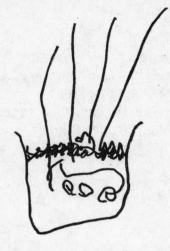

Materials
1. 4–6 bamboo shoots from a nursery
2. Small clean rocks or pebbles
3. Glass or ceramic vase

Directions
Place the rocks or pebbles in the container to about one-third of the height. Trim the bamboo shoots top and bottom. Place the shoots firmly into the rocks. Fill vase with water and place on a window ledge or coffee table. Change the water weekly and watch your oriental garden grow.

avocado tree

Materials
1. Avocado seed
2. Sharp nail
3. 3 toothpicks
4. Small water tumbler

Directions

Make three holes in the avocado seed with a sharp nail. Insert a toothpick in each hole and make sure they are secure. Fill glass tumbler with water and balance the avocado seed on top using the toothpicks. The tip of the seed should be in the water. Place the cup on a window ledge. Soon a root and a shoot will appear. As soon as the shoot has leaves, snip off the top. This will let the avocado tree branch out. Pot the little tree when roots are thick (a few weeks). Continue to snip off the top growth to make a thicker bush.

tree family

Directions
Take a look around your yard. If you have a space to plant a few trees, consider buying trees that are the height of each person in your family. Plant them in a group and measure them yearly. Compare how fast the person grows compared to the trees. Notice how the adult's trees grow while the adults do not grow. Depending on the age of the child, the tree may grow slower or faster. Let each person name his or her tree.

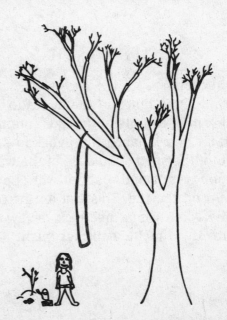

spring is here

Materials
1. 6 daffodil bulbs or
   6 crocus bulbs
2. 5" clay or plastic pot
3. Potting soil

Directions

Moisten the potting soil and half fill the five-inch pot with some soil. Place the bulbs on the soil and then add more soil until the tips of the bulbs just peek through. The crocus bulbs should be planted close together. Sprinkle with water and set the pot somewhere cool and dark. Check the bulbs every couple of days and keep moist. After three weeks they will have roots and green shoots. Bring them out into the sunlight and continue to keep the soil moist. After a month, they will bloom and it will seem as though spring has arrived. Bulbs will grow faster if kept in the fridge for a week or so before planting.

outdoor terrarium

Materials
1. 2 or 3 wide-mouthed jars
2. Vegetable and flower seeds—dwarf varieties
3. Fertilizer
4. Garden or planter space

Directions
Wash and dry the jars and remove any labels. Locate a small piece of garden or an empty planter. Remove weeds and stones and dig over the soil. Mix in a little fertilizer. Sow the seeds in an area no larger than the size of the mouth of each jar. Space jars about twelve inches apart. Cover seeds with soil and sprinkle with water. Place jar over the seeds and watch them germinate inside their terrarium or hothouse. The jars protect the seeds from extremes of temperatures. Remove jars to water the seedlings. When the seedlings are strong and healthy, remove the jar permanently.

mr. potato

Materials
1. Medium-size potato
2. Pipe cleaners
3. Toothpicks
4. Modeling clay

Directions
Scrub and then dry the potato. Break the toothpicks (about six of them) in two. Take the modeling clay and shape into noses, ears, mouths, eyebrows, and eyeballs. Use several colors. To create a potato head, push the blunt end of the toothpick into one of the clay shapes. Now insert the sharp end into the potato at the place where your child thinks it should go. Continue attaching the clay facial features until the head is complete. Use the pipe cleaners to make arms and legs. Mr. Potato can have different faces according to your child's imagination.

crocus garden

Materials
1. 8–10 crocus bulbs
2. Empty cardboard ice cream carton
3. Potting soil

Directions

Cut 8–10 holes in the sides of an ice cream carton. Poke smaller holes in the base for drainage. They should be about one inch in diameter. Carefully pack the moistened potting soil into the carton and each time you come to a hole in the side, place a crocus bulb near it. Press the soil down firmly to keep it from spilling out of the holes. Leave one inch to spare at the top. Place the carton in a cool dark place for six weeks, checking weekly to see that the soil is moist. Bring the carton into the sunlight and allow the green leaves to protrude through the holes. The crocuses will bloom in about a month.

greenhouse in the round

Materials
1. Spherical glass jar or vase
2. Gravel or small pebbles
3. Potting mix or fine garden soil
4. Indoor plant seedlings

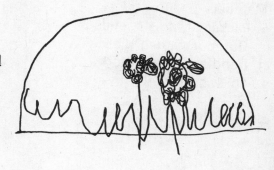

Directions
Clean and rinse the round glass container. Put a layer of gravel or pebbles in the base and then added potting soil to a depth of two or three inches. Moisten the soil. Carefully transplant the seedlings into the soil and press the soil down gently around the roots. Place the container in indirect sunlight and keep the soil moist, but not soggy. Trim the plants if they become too tall, and enjoy the miniature greenhouse.

rows of radishes

Materials
1. Packet of radish seeds
2. Outdoor garden plot
3. Hand shovel and fork
4. Thick stick

Directions
Find a small area of the garden and begin by preparing the soil. Your child first removes stones, weeds, and other debris. Turn the soil over with the shovel and crumble it in your hands so that it is fine. With the stick, your child next draws several straight lines. Sow the radish seeds in the rows (about a half-inch deep) and cover with soil. Sprinkle the rows with water and pat them down firmly. In less than three weeks, the radishes will be ready to harvest. Wash thoroughly before eating.

flowering names

Materials
1. Wildflower seeds
2. Stick
3. Garden plot

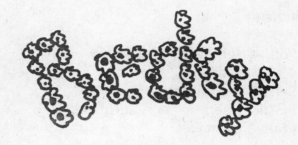

Directions
Prepare the soil of a section of the garden—about 4 x 3 feet. Remove stones, weeds, and other debris. Smooth the dirt. Using the stick, write your child's name in the soil, making the groove one inch deep. Evenly sprinkle the wildflower seeds into the lines. Press the dirt into the grooves with your hands or the edge of the stick. Even before the plants flower, your child will be able to discern her name as the seedlings appear. You could also make a flower picture.

life in the desert

Materials
1. Tray
2. Potting soil mixed with sand
3. 6 small cacti
4. Small hand mirror
5. Plastic desert animals, such as camels, lizards, or snakes

Directions
Spread the soil and sand mixture in the tray. Plant the cactus plants in the soil according to directions. Sprinkle very lightly with water. Place the mirror in the sand to create a mirage and put the animals among the cacti. To find out when to water your desert, check the weather conditions for Arizona in the newspaper. Whenever it rains in Arizona, that is when you water your cactus plants.

carrot baskets

Materials
1. A really fat carrot
2. 3 paper clips
3. Heavy thread or string

Directions
Remove the leaves from the carrot. Cut a three-inch piece from the top (fat end) of the carrot, lay it on the counter, and scoop out some of the insides to make a bowl shape. Open up the paper clips and push the straight end into the carrot about one-half inch from the top of the bowl. Cut thread into three twelve-inch lengths and tie each one to a paper clip. Knot them together at the other end. Fill the carrot's bowl with water and hang in a sunny place, such as in front of the kitchen window. Soon the carrot's leaves will grow back and form a green basket.

surprise nut tree

Materials
1. Walnut shells
2. Ribbon
3. Small tree branch
4. Tiny surprises to put into walnut shells
5. Used plastic pot with soil in it

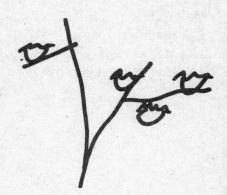

Directions
Fill the walnut shells with tiny surprises, such as M&Ms, nuts, raisins, or folded-up notes and fortunes. Glue or tape the shells together and tie a length of ribbon around each one. Push the branch into the soil in the pot so that it is secure. Tie the shells to the branch by the ribbons so they hang free. Your child can snip the ribbon with scissors and open the shells to find out what's inside.

elf garden

Materials
1. Foil pie plate
2. Soil
3. Moss
4. Hand mirror
5. Tiny plants, ferns, or seedlings

Directions
Pack some soil into the pie plate. Proceed to make a simple garden of small proportions. Use the moss to give contours. Place the mirror on the soil to make a pond. Insert the plants around the mirror and between the clumps of moss. Keep moist by sprinkling lightly with water. Keep out of direct sunlight. Imagine the elves who might live there.

tiny basket planter

Materials
1. Plastic berry container
2. Ribbons
3. Potting soil
4. Seeds
5. Foil

Directions
Weave ribbons in and out of basket spaces until all spaces are filled. Line basket with some foil. Fill with potting soil and moisten. Sprinkle seeds on top of soil and press down. Cover basket with plastic until seeds germinate. Water often with a fine spray. Basket can be hung or placed on a window ledge.

leaf log

Materials
1. Paper bag
2. Heavy book
3. Scotch tape
4. Blank page notebook

Directions
On a fine day, go walking with your child and collect leaves. Fresh leaves are best. Put them in the paper bag. When you get home, press the leaves between absorbent paper (coffee filters are best) in a heavy book. Leave for a day or two. Remove the pressed leaves from the book and attach them to the blank pages of the notebook with Scotch tape. Try to identify each leaf and then write its name on the page. Build the leaf log by taking walks to different places or by collecting leaves seasonally.

make-believe

ghost land

Materials
1. Open space that has been cleared of dangerous objects
2. Old sheet

Directions
Create an imaginary ghost land. First, clear an area of any objects one might run into, or plan on doing this activity outside on a warm evening. Explain to your child how she is going to pretend to be a ghost by putting a sheet over her head and then wandering around in the open space. Cover your child with an old sheet and lead her into the middle of the space. Now watch the creative ideas and movements evolve from your child's imagination. Encourage the idea of friendly, funny, singing ghosts. Make sure to remain in the room so that if your child wanders the wrong direction you can bring her back into the safe area. Afterwards, talk about what it feels like to be unable to see where you are going. If your child is afraid of ghosts, take this opportunity to explain how this is a made-up idea, just like your child is now pretending to be a ghost.

mail delivery

Materials
1. A cloth grocery bag or old purse
2. Junk mail
3. Old shoe boxes
4. Markers

Directions
Create mailboxes for family members out of the old shoe boxes. Write each person's name at the end of the box and decorate with markers. When junk mail arrives, write the name of family members on the back of the letters. Put the junk mail in the bag and ask your child to deliver the mail to the homemade mailboxes according to the names written on the back. As your child get older and is able to read real address labels, let her collect and sort the family mail.

peek-a-boo box

Materials
1. Shoe box with lid
2. Scissors
3. Glue
4. Tape
5. Colored paper, clay, shells, feathers, miniature toys, pictures

Directions
Cut out a window in one end of the box and another window of similar size in the lid. Inside the box, create a scene or theme. With the lid off, glue or tape objects and pictures to the bottom and sides. Use modeling clay to affix objects like feathers and miniature toys, so they stand upright. Place the other small objects so they can be seen through both windows. Replace the lid and look through each window to view the diorama. Talk about how different the scene looks from above versus looking from the side.

dressing up

Materials

1. Large cardboard carton or wooden crate
2. Old adult clothes
3. Bags, purses, wallets
4. Hats, ties, shoes, belts
5. Scarves, shawls, and other used accessories

Directions

Today is a good day to start a dress-up bin for your child. Go through your closet, and instead of discarding your old clothes, put some of them in a box or crate for your child to play with. Keep adding to the box as your wardrobe changes. When your child wants to dress up, make a full-length mirror available and have your camera or video camera ready. Since the clothes fit you too, don't forget to join in the fun.

a day at the lake

Materials
1. Sack lunch
2. Long stick
3. String
4. Magnet
5. Small metal objects—
   bottle caps, keys, etc.
6. Blanket

Directions
Regardless of the weather, make-believe that you and your child are going on a fishing trip. Prepare sack lunches and gather the other materials. Find a spot inside or outside the house and spread the blanket. Imagine you are by a lake in the woods. To make a fishing pole, tie the string to one end of the stick and tie the magnet to the other. Spread the small metal objects around you or drop them into a box or basket. Relax as you fish with your child and eat lunch together.

is it a bird, or a bat, or a butterfly?

Materials
1. An old sheet or tablecloth
2. Felt markers or paints
3. Preferably a windy day

Directions

Take the old sheet or tablecloth and make it into a large cape for your child. Do this by cutting it to fit. Hold the edge of the sheet up to your child's chin, then mark the sheet four to six inches up from the floor so that the cape won't drag. Spread it out on a flat surface and trim away the bottom. Let your child decorate the cape with colored markings or paints. Attach wrist loops to the corners if your child would find it easier to hold the cape that way. You can make wrist loops by sewing a piece of ribbon or seam binding on the corner, then tying the ribbon around your child's wrist. Or make the loops out of elastic. Go outside on a windy day and let your child run into the wind, imagining that he is a bird, bat, butterfly—or anything else that flies.

pantomime play

Directions

Discuss some of the everyday actions your child does, such as drinking milk, brushing teeth, putting on socks and shoes, and climbing stairs. One of you reenact these activities silently and with exaggeration, letting the other guess what you are acting out. Make up some other activities to act out, like picking flowers, riding a horse, or going to the store. The pantomime can be real or imaginary as long as you are acting it out in silence.

tiny yarn doll story

Materials
1. Ball of yarn
2. Heavy cardboard—6" tall
3. Scissors

Directions
Take the cardboard frame and wind the yarn around it thirty times. Slip a piece of string under one end of the frame and tie. Cut the yarn at the other end and remove the frame. Tie a little off at around the one-and-a-half-inch mark at the top to form a head. Remove the original string and detach two small clusters to form the arms and tie them at the wrists. Tie a string around the waist. Separate the remaining yarn into two legs. Tie at the ankles. Invent a story about the adventures of your tiny yarn doll.

cloud associations

Directions
This activity is to be done on a day when there are clouds in the sky, otherwise find a photography book with photos of the sky. Start by explaining how clouds are formed, then take turns pointing out different cloud shapes and patterns. Ask your child what each cloud's shape makes her think about and why. Or start putting together an imaginary story about the cloud shapes, a family of clouds in the sky, or a world of sky creatures. This activity is best done when lying on your backs and looking upwards.

magic wand

Materials
1. Long stick or dowel
2. Fabric scraps or crepe paper
3. Sequins
4. Gift bow
5. Glue

Directions

Help your child make a magic wand she can use to create spells, make people disappear, and grant that wishes come true. Wrap the stick in strips of colorful fabric or crepe paper. Glue on some sequins. Attach a gift bow or streamers to the top. Let your child come up with decorations that would make her wand special: a lock of her doll's hair, a special ribbon she wore on her birthday, a small picture, rocks, or beads. Let it dry. Now the wand is ready for its magical use.

woman in the moon

Directions
One night when the moon is up, lie with your child on your backs on a blanket or lounge chair in the backyard. Look up at the moon and the night sky. What do you see? Can you connect the stars to make a picture? Can you make out a face on the moon? Imagine what it would be like to be an astronaut flying into space in a rocket. What would you expect to find on the moon? What would you do there? How would you feel about being so far away from Earth?

space weaving

Materials
1. Yarn
2. String
3. Things to hang

Directions

Sometimes bedrooms—or rooms, for that matter—get boring. When that happens it's time to create an imaginary space: maybe a jungle, a haunted house, a rabbit's burrow, or an inhabitable planet. Start by attaching some yarn or string to the doorknob and then taking it around the room and the furniture, wrapping it under furniture and stretching it high towards the ceiling. Continue to crisscross the room until a web-like structure has been created. Now weave ribbons, scarves, and more yarn in and out of the space. Hang or tie objects that go with the theme. Depending on how much of the room is covered by your space weaving, leave it up for a few days to enjoy and play within.

vacation at home

Directions
When you're thinking about time off, don't ignore the option of staying home and doing something unusual. Get everybody together to plan a mini-vacation at home. It's tricky because you'll need to pretend you are somewhere else while you're at home. For this purpose, give your home the name of a hotel. Select restaurants in the area where you'll be eating. Choose nearby places of interest or events to attend. Don't do any routine chores. Think about hiring a teenage neighbor to provide maid service while you're out. Unplug the phone. Call out for pizza and pretend it's room service. Send postcards to friends and relatives. Take pictures. Vacations are for having fun, no matter where you are.

i am a fish

Materials
1. Blue construction paper
2. Photo of child's face
3. Glue
4. Sand
5. Brushes
6. Tape
7. Crayons or felt pens

Directions
Create a story about living and swimming at the bottom of the sea. Prepare the bottom of the sea by brushing glue onto the blue paper. Sprinkle sand on the paper and wait until the glue dries. Pour off the excess sand. In one of the spaces, glue your child's photo. Using crayons or felt pens, draw a fish's body and tail using the photo in place of a fish's face. Have your child draw other sea creatures and seaweed. Use more blue paper if necessary. Pretend you are like the fish in the picture, swimming around in a sea of blue surrounded by your sea friends.

storybook videos

Directions

Gather a few of your favorite storybooks and prepare to videotape yourself or your child reading them. Make sure to show your child how you read the page first and then hold it up for the camera to zoom in on. This is like storybook hour in the library, but you get to watch this video whenever you'd like. The next time you have a grandparent or other relative visit, ask them to videotape a book reading. Or have your child make a book reading and send it to his grandparents.

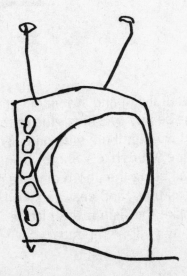

magic movies

Materials
1. Adding machine paper, or similar roll 2 to 3 inches in width.
2. Matchbox (from large kitchen matches)
3. Crayons

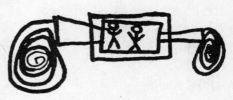

Directions
Ask your child to draw a story along the tape. It should look somewhat like a comic strip. A series of shapes or pictures would work too. Cut out a square in the side of the matchbox to serve as the viewing area. Decorate the matchbox to look like a viewing screen. Thread the tape through the box so that the child's pictures appear in the window. Place the box on a table and wind and unwind the tape through the box.

candy castle

Materials
1. Boxes, cardboard cylinders
2. All types of candy and cookies
3. Ice cream cones (V-shaped)
4. Duct tape
5. Frosting

Frosting recipe
1. 3 egg whites
2. 4 to 4-½ cups confectioners' sugar

Using an electric mixer, beat the egg whites until they form stiff peaks. Add four cups of the confectioners' sugar one cup at a time and continue beating until smooth. For a stiffer frosting, add additional sugar.

Directions
Assemble the boxes, cylinders, and cones in the shape of a castle. Duct tape the pieces together so that once the icing is applied the structure will be solid and won't move around. Spread icing on one part of the castle at a time, sticking candy, cookies, and decorations on as you go.

stand-up drawings

Materials
1. Poster board, used cartons, or boxes
2. Pencil
3. Crayons
4. Scissors

Directions
Have your child draw some simple shapes: trees, houses, people, and animals. Cut around the drawing, leaving a one-inch space beneath each drawing that can be folded over so that the shape stands when finished. Fold the shapes at their bases and stand them up. Have your child arrange the stand-up drawings into a scene for a make-believe story. Participate in the story and be prepared to add more shapes as the story evolves.

early native american weaving

Materials
1. V-shaped branch
2. Yarn or string
3. Collected objects from nature—
   feathers, shells, grasses,
   flowers, roots, etc.

Directions
Make-believe that you and your child are early Native Americans and go for a nature walk. While you are walking, talk what life might have been like before there were houses and lots of people living in big cities. Most native tribes did some sort of weaving. Collect objects that the Native Americans may have found. Find a fallen V-shaped branch and wrap the string or yarn around the branch to make a loom. Weave, hang, and tie in the objects that you found. Take the branch home with you for family and friends to admire.

tent time

Materials
1. Blankets
2. Furniture

Directions

Before you start this activity, remove all precious ornaments, dangerous furniture, and potted plants from the room. Provide your child with three or four blankets and facilitate the construction of a huge tent. Drape the blankets over the furniture. When the tent is finished, encourage your child to play a make-believe game, such as being in a circus, a haunted house, a fort, or a magic forest.

switching roles

Directions
This activity requires that you and your child switch roles for the day (or part of the day). Explain to the rest of the household what is happening and ask for their cooperation. If more convenient, your child could pretend to be another member of the family—a sibling or grandparent. The make-believe could include duties, clothes, behaviors, vocabulary, and other habits. Keep the activity positive and fun.

my own story

Materials
1. Notebook
2. Pen or pencil
3. Crayons

Directions
In this activity, your child will think of a story and while he tells it to you, you will record it in a notebook. Leave every alternate page blank for your child's illustrations that he can draw after the story is complete. Read the story back to your child and be prepared for additions and elaborations. Save the book of stories for when your child is older.

new endings

Materials

1. Favorite storybooks

Directions

The object of this activity is to read a familiar story to your child with a made-up ending. It's important to choose a favorite story so your child will know what the ending is supposed to be. When you are near the end, stop and have your child finish the story by inventing a new ending. It can be funny, sad, dramatic, or silly. The same story can have several endings. Repeat this activity with another story.

act it out

Materials

1. An adventure story

Directions

Read your child an exciting adventure story. When you have finished, plan to reenact it with suggestions from your child for props and scenes. Use chairs, cushions, and other furniture to set the stage. Involve other members of the family if needed. Act out the story in front of an audience or just between yourselves.

pirates and gypsies

Materials

1. Bandanas
2. Black construction paper
3. Rubber bands or elastic
4. White or silver paper
5. Scissors
6. Necklaces or strings of beads

Directions

In order to play pirates and gypsies, it is necessary to prepare the costumes—scarves, eye patches, necklaces, and earrings. To make the eye patches, cut a circle out of the black paper and thread rubber bands through the sides so that they stretch around your child's head. Cut a circle out of white or silver paper and cut out the inside, leaving a width of half an inch. Slash the ring and hook it around or onto your child's ear. Lastly, tie the bandana around her head and drape the necklaces.

up the hill

Directions
Take your child to a grassy slope. Explore the different ways he can climb the slope and then come down again. Try to do it the way animals might: birds, grasshoppers, elephants, worms, and monkeys. Go up like one animal and come down like another. Or try going up fast and coming down slowly. Think of other imaginative ways you and your child can enjoy the incline.

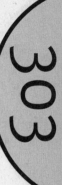

stay off the sidewalk cracks!

Directions
This make-believe activity can be played anywhere there are patterns on the ground or floor. Children are told that they are only "safe" when their feet are not touching the cracks or seams or lines on the ground or floor. Use the child's imagination to decide the object from which they need to be protected. This activity can also be done on a jungle gym or outdoor play structure when to be "safe" would mean to stay off the ground.

grandma and grandpa

Materials
1. Large sheet of white paper
2. Pencil or black pen
3. Photos of grandparents

Directions
Have your child recount a story about her grandparent(s). It could be something your child has actually experienced or something she would like to. Write down what your child tells you on the paper. When you have finished with the story, illustrate it with drawings and photos. Fold it neatly and then send it to the lucky grandparent(s).

music

spray drums

Materials

1. Garden hose
2. Spray attachment (for hose)
3. Metal or plastic pots, pans, lids, bowls
4. Grassy space or level driveway

Directions

Turn the pots and pans upside down on the grass or driveway. Lean some of the larger lids or pans against a wall, bench, or tree. Attach the sprayer to the hose and turn on the water. Have the child spray the metal objects with water to make drumming sounds and rhythms. Experiment with varying intensities of water force—from dripping to torrential. Take frequent breaks to rearrange pots, pans, and lids for various sound effects.

change a song

Directions

Children like to sing about the familiar things in their lives—family, school, toys, going to bed, mealtimes, siblings, and feelings. Take a well-known melody such as "Twinkle, Twinkle, Little Star" and have your child make up new words to the song. Create many variations. Nonsense words with lots of repetition are fun and easy for the youngest child. Rhyming doesn't matter. Take turns so that everyone has an opportunity to make up a new song.

maraca march

Materials
1. Plastic bottles with long necks, like ketchup and sauce bottles
2. Rice, beans, bird seed
3. Macaroni
4. Masking tape

Directions
Partly fill the bottles with rice, beans, bird seed, or macaroni. Seal the bottles with masking tape. Wrap additional tape around the necks to make a comfortable handle. Make a pair for each child. Now encourage your child to move and shake the "maracas" either to music, hands clapping, or no sounds at all. Marching is a good activity to start with, which can be developed into other locomotive motions like skipping, galloping, leaping, hopping, and stamping as the child becomes more creative and comfortable moving around while playing the handheld rhythmic instruments. Let your child shake out a rhythm while you dance, then you shake while she dances. Add drums or other instruments to accompany the maracas.

rainstick

Materials
- 1½- to 3-inch wide mailing tube
- 1 lb. of 1½-inch nails (or 3-inch nails)
- 1 hammer
- Wide plastic tape, or plastic tube stopper
- Funnel
- Selection of sand, rice, lentils, popcorn kernels, dried beans
- Paint, construction paper, markers, or crayons for decoration

Directions
Show your child how to hammer the nails into the tube. Let him place the nails wherever he likes. Once the entire pound of nails have been used, seal one end of the tube with the plastic stopper or tape. Use a funnel to pour a test amount of rice or beans into the tube, and have your child seal the open end with one hand while he experiments with sounds. Once he decides what the contents of his tubes will be, seal both ends securely. Decorate however you like.

wrist and ankle jingles

Materials
1. ½ yard of narrow ribbon
2. 6 or more small bells

Directions
Cut ribbon into six- to eight-inch lengths. String the bells onto the ribbon—about three bells to each length. Tie knots between the bells and at each end of the ribbon to keep them in place. Tie ribbons loosely around your child's wrists and ankles. Try walking, running, hopping, and jumping while you listen to the different jingling sounds that are produced. Also try different arm and hand movements and see what kind of rhythms the various movements create. Turn on music and jingle to the beat.

accompanying the dance

Materials
1. Toy musical instruments
2. Homemade musical instruments

Directions
Begin this activity by having your child improvise a tune on each of the musical instruments you've gathered. The adult can listen attentively or, better still, can dance to the sounds the child is making. Then change roles. The adult plays the instruments and the child dances to them. If there are two children, one can play while the other dances. The sounds of each instrument should suggest the movements, and as the child moves, appropriate sounds should be produced that accompany the dance as well. Notice the difference when you make music to go along with the dance versus dancing with the music.

sounds alive

Materials
1. Soft objects (stuffed toys, pillows, slippers)
2. Hollow objects (pots, cans, egg cartons, plastic bottles)
3. Solid objects (books, stones, bricks, blocks)

Directions
Different shapes and densities produce different sounds. Make sounds on and with the objects using your hands and fingers. Listen to the sounds. Explain to your child that soft sounds and slow sounds are as interesting as loud and fast sounds, and that quiet times are as nice as noisy times. Try a quiet time. Close your eyes and listen to the sounds in your thoughts and imagination. Talk about what these sounds are like—soft, loud, slow, or fast?

sanded blocks

Materials
1. Sandpaper
2. 2 wooden blocks or pieces of wood the size of a blackboard eraser
3. Masking tape and ribbon

Directions
Cut the sandpaper so that it fits over the wooden block and overlaps slightly. Tape it securely to the block. Use thumbtacks if preferred. Make loops out of the ribbon and attach it to the blocks so that your child can hang them from his wrists. This makes it easier to dance and play at the same time. To make sounds, rub the blocks together. They can be clapped together and tapped too. Play silly, fun music and accompany it with the sanded blocks. Try tapping your feet, stomping, and marching to echo the rhythm being made by the blocks. Remember to keep all your handmade instruments so that when friends are over, you can form a band.

sound count

Materials
1. Dice

Directions
Here's a game that helps a younger child learn numbers and an older child learn how to count to a beat. Roll a die. Whatever number shows up on the die determines the number of sounds your child needs to make. These sounds can be made by clapping, humming, singing, or playing various musical instruments. The fun of this game comes in stringing the various sounds together as the non-sound-making participant counts. Take turns. Help your child count the number of sounds by saying a number as his sound is made.

exploring sound

Directions

Set aside a quiet time when you and your child can sit and listen to the sounds around you. Begin by simply trying to identify what you hear. Distinguish between the sounds inside the house and the sounds coming from outside the house. Or the sounds that are close and the ones that are far away. Also, pick out the loudest sounds and the softest sounds. Listen to the sounds of your breathing and of your eyelashes blinking. Share what you hear.

jingle bell drum

Materials
1. Oatmeal carton (cylinder)
2. 24 inches of sturdy string
3. Glue
4. 2 packages of small sleigh bells
5. Colored paper, wallpaper, or fabric
6. Tape

Directions
Stiffen one end of the string with glue and let it dry. This will make threading the bells easier. String the bells onto the string, making large knots between them to keep them from touching each other. Cover the oatmeal carton with colorful paper and glue it on securely. Attach the strung bells to the carton with the tape, starting at the top and then winding the string in a spiral fashion towards the bottom. Attach the string along the bottom rim. Now the portable drum is ready for shaking or tapping.

nail melodies

Materials
1. A variety of large and small nails
2. Thread, preferably nylon
3. A tall-backed chair or clothes drying rack

Directions
Tie different lengths of thread to the nail heads. Hang the nails from the back of a chair, the rungs of a clothes drying rack, or a stepladder. Nails could also be hung from bathroom towel holders. Use a large nail, fondue fork, or thin dowel to strike nails. Try fast and slow, loud and soft sounds. Other metal objects can be tied and hung for more variety. Use radio music or other music for accompaniment.

drum echoes

Materials
1. Two toy or homemade drums
2. Mallet or padded drumsticks

Directions
Play a simple rhythm on the drum and have the child listen carefully to it. Start with three or fewer beats. Ask your child to repeat the pattern (or "message"). Continue to listen and repeat the rhythmic phrases. Next, have the child create an original pattern with the adult trying to copy it. Allow the drum talking and answering to proceed spontaneously.

wind chime magic

Directions

The sound of the wind moving through bells, seashells, beads, stones, or tumbled glass reminds us of the movement of nature—it places our attention for just one moment someplace magical. Go on a treasure hunt looking for items that create a pretty sound when they collide with each other—look around the house, in the garden, at the beach, or in craft stores.

Wind chimes are unique creations because they can be made of so many different things. Three components are necessary to make a wind chime—string, sound makers, and some solid structure that holds everything together. Pieces of wood, sticks, plastic lids, even old toys make good solid structures.

Take string or nylon thread and attach the sound-makers to the solid structure by pushing a hole through it, wrapping the thread around and tying it, or by securing with tape. Loop the string at the top so the wind chime can be hung from a nail on a roof overhang just above the deck.

bottle tooting

Materials
1. Empty glass bottles with narrow tops
2. Water

Directions

Pour water into each bottle so the water hits each bottle in a different spot. To make the bottle "toot," blow straight across the open top. Try short breaths and long breaths. Then alternate short and long breaths. Hold the bottle against your lower lip and see how long your child can "toot." Make up a duet, with each of you playing one or two bottles, or invite others to participate and form a "tooting" band.

snare drum

Materials
1. Empty cookie or cake tin
2. 20 paper clips
3. Cardboard
4. Masking tape

Directions
Remove the lid from the empty tin. Turn the tin upside down and cut a piece of cardboard the same size as the tin bottom (use the lid to trace around). Set the tin right-side up and put the paper clips on the recessed bottom. Put the cardboard on the top and secure with masking tape. Use chopsticks or pencils to play on the cardboard.

sounds like?

Directions
The idea of this activity is to imitate the everyday sounds we hear with our voices. It can be done inside or outside the house—just walk around and listen. Try imitating such sounds as a door shutting, the telephone ringing, the washing machine or dryer, the teakettle whistling, the fire crackling, and the fridge humming. Repeat outside with sounds such as birds chirping, leaves rustling, sirens, brakes squealing, and planes overhead. Who knows, you might have a sound-effects person in the making!

bongo drums

Materials
1. 3 different size cylinders with plastic lids (oatmeal containers, bread crumbs, or coffee cans)
2. Masking tape
3. String

Ponk
Ponk
Ponk

Directions

Tape and then tie the cylinders together to make a set of bongo drums. Set the drums on the child's lap and briefly demonstrate how to beat each drum with the fingers, palms, knuckles, and heels of the hands, creating a variety of sounds and rhythms.

clapping rhythms

Directions
Try this rhythmic game with your child. All you need is some space and a low noise level. As your child walks around, clap each time he takes a step. Encourage your child to run, hop, jump, gallop, and skip, and continue to clap out the rhythm his steps make. For a change of perspective, have your child clap out the stepping rhythms that you make—but be sure to keep them reasonably slow, regular, and simple. After you try clapping with the feet as they touch the ground, try clapping and making the feet touch the ground to the clapped rhythm.

finger tapping

Materials
1. 10 thimbles or acorn caps
2. Small Band-Aids
3. Old pair of children's gloves
4. Buttons

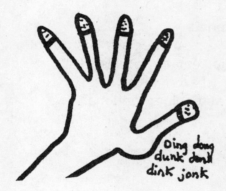

Ding dong
dunk donk
dink jonk

Directions
Place the thimbles or acorn caps on your child's fingers. To make sure they fit snugly, secure with the small Band-Aids. Begin tapping with the fingertips on a table or a non-carpeted floor. Now experiment with other surfaces—stone, metal, marble, plastic, Formica, ceramic. Listen to the different sounds that each surface produces. If you have an old pair of children's gloves, you can glue larger-size thimbles onto the ends of the fingers or simply sew buttons on. Then you will have permanent "finger tapping" gloves for your child.

musical jar xylophone

Materials
1. 10–12 empty glass jars or bottles
2. Homemade "drumsticks"
3. Pitcher of water
4. Food colors (optional)

Directions
Arrange the jars or bottles on a flat, low surface. Pour water into the jars in varying amounts and add drops of food color. Provide your child with a selection of drumsticks: pencil, wooden spoon, or chopsticks. Encourage him to explore the various sounds and rhythms that can be produced by tapping the jars. Try tapping the jars below the water line, then above it, and notice if the sound changes. Hum a tune and encourage your child to tap along.

copycat music

Materials

1. Musical instruments with notes—piano, xylophone, harmonica, or guitar

Directions

Sit back-to-back with your child. Play a few notes on the instrument. Ask her to hum or sing them back to you. Start with familiar nursery rhymes, holiday songs, or well-known jingles if you can play them, otherwise a group of notes is fine. After a while, give your child the instrument and see if you can copy the notes that she produces. If you do not have access to musical instruments, sing the notes and phrases with your own voice.

zoo and farm sounds

Materials

1. A story about visiting the zoo or a farm from a storybook, or make one up as you go along

Directions

Read the story to your child and explain that each time an animal is mentioned you will stop reading for a moment while she makes the sounds of the animal. Read it a second time through and this time have your child sing a short melody (to a recognized song like "Twinkle, Twinkle, Little Star") using animal sounds.

child's own operetta

Directions
With your child, make up a make-believe story that involves animals, nature sounds, and favorite storybook characters. As you tell the story together, sing some of the words and have your child make all the sound effects. Include movements that seem appropriate and fun too.

only a song

Directions
You and your child are going to play a game of songs. You will sing everything to him instead of talking. He has to sing back. The quality of your singing isn't of concern. The important thing is to sing everything: questions, answers, conversation, and directives. For example, sing, "How are you this morning?" and, "Are you ready for breakfast?" If the other person doesn't sing back you can pretend that you don't hear them.

Nice day

louder, softer please

Directions

Sing a favorite song. Start singing it loud and gradually sing more softly as if the song were moving off into the distance. Sing some more of the song, this time getting louder and louder as if the song were moving towards you. This little exercise helps your child to understand the dynamics of sound and music. Try picking a new song and change the volume to suit the words and meaning of the song.

story soundtrack

humpy Dumpty

Directions

Pick a favorite storybook that happens to have action that might be associated with a certain sound, like rain, footsteps, wind, a train whistle, or a crackling fire. Or write your own story with some of these elements.

To create rain, spray water from the sink sprayer into a bowl of water or run the shower into a bucket.

For footsteps, go outside and walk on gravel, or fill a box with sand or gravel and walk in place. Create the sound of running the same way.

For the sound of a fire, crumple up an empty potato chip bag.
You can purchase train whistles in hobby stores.

Be creative with all the sounds you come up with. Record the sounds in the order you would hear them in the book. Then, as each sound is read, you can turn on the tape. It is also fun to have the sound effect makers right at hand so you can add them live as the story is read.

kazoo flute

Materials
1. Cardboard tube from paper towel
2. Wax paper
3. Rubber band
4. Pencil or knitting needle
5. Paints

Directions

Paint or decorate the tube and let dry. With the pencil, punch three to five holes in the tube in a line and only through one side. Cover one end with the waxed paper and secure with the rubber band. Hum against the wax paper and use the fingers on the holes to vary the sound.

paint a song

Materials
1. Butcher paper
2. Crayons, markers, or paints
3. Taped or recorded music

Directions
Sit on the floor with your child and spread a large piece of the butcher paper between you. Have the crayons, markers, and paints handy and ready to use. Put on some music and close your eyes for a minute or so to get the "feel" of the sound and rhythm. Open your eyes and draw the music as you hear it. The drawings should reflect the rhythm, dynamics, tempo, and mood of the music rather than represent the person, place, or thing.

bottle-top castanets

Materials
1. Cardboard
2. 4 bottle caps

Directions
Cut cardboard into two eight-inch strips. Fold each strip in half and glue a bottle cap to each end on the inside. To use the castanets, the child holds a folded cardboard strip in each hand with the bottle caps facing. The bottle caps will click together when the hands are opened and closed.

nature

walking collector

Materials
1. Bottle of glue with brush
2. Strong cardboard
3. Empty egg carton or shoe box

Directions
Go for a walk outside with your child. Stop to look at leaves, bark, flowers, stones, feathers, or other items you see in nature. You can either create your art piece while walking by gluing found objects onto the board as you go, or you can design your piece once you return home by putting the found objects in the egg carton to be attached later. Talk about each object: what your child likes about it, the color, texture, smell, and how it came to be where you found it.

sand saucers

Materials
1. Sand or fine dirt
2. Old saucers or foil plates
3. Flowers, leaves, seeds
4. Buttons, shells, feathers, and other small objects

Directions
Fill a saucer, plate, or disposable foil pie tin with damp sand and mound slightly. Press the flowers and other small objects into the sand, making a design or mandala. Encourage your child to create a small land where fairies might live, or perhaps a secret garden for insects. Try using various objects to trace a design on the surface of the sand to create a Zen garden. Sand saucers last a couple of days if sand is kept moist. They make interesting table decorations or garden display pieces.

stone reflections

Materials
1. Assorted stones and pebbles
2. Glass jar
3. Bleach

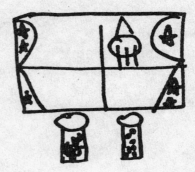

Directions
Gather different colored stones and pebbles with your child. When you get home, wash them and then carefully put them in the jar. Fill the jar with water and add a teaspoon of bleach to keep the water clear. Place the jar where the light catches it and look at the colors that are reflected. Explain that the bleach keeps the water clean so that the stones and pebbles look clean and bright. Remind your child not to put his fingers in the water.

mud play

Materials
1. Garden soil
2. Piece of plastic

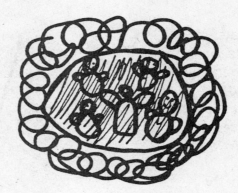

Directions
All children like the feel of mud. Make a hole in the ground and save the pile of dirt. Line the hole with the sheet of plastic, then fill the hole back up with the dirt and water. Your child can simply squish the mud through her fingers or make whatever shapes or figures she wants. It's also fun to put your feet in the hole to feel mud squish through your toes. After the activity is over, hose the area down (and your child too!).

pet worm

Materials
1. Glass jar
2. Garden soil
3. Sand
4. Peat (optional)
5. Leaves
6. Live worm

Directions
To make the wormery, put a layer of soil at the bottom of the jar. Add a layer of sand, a layer of peat, and finally, a layer of leaves. Place the worm on top of the leaves and then wrap paper around the jar to keep it dark. After a few days, remove the paper and show your child how the layers have begun to get mixed up due to the worm's movements and eating habits.

fall fun

Materials
1. Leaf rake
2. Child's wagon

Directions
When there is a layer of leaves on the ground, take your child outside for some fall fun. Rake the leaves into small piles and play, chasing around and in between the piles. Or try leaping over them. Using the wagon, cart the leaves to make one big pile. Try to run through it or sit your child in the way and pull him through the leaves. Try burying each other in leaves, catching the leaves as they fall, and sorting them into colors and shapes.

rock crystals

Materials
1. Porous stones or charcoal briquettes
2. Vinegar
3. Salt
4. Warm water
5. Food color (optional)
6. Small enamel or glass bowl

Directions
Add three tablespoons of salt to half a bowl of warm water and stir until it dissolves. Keep adding salt until no more will dissolve. Add a tablespoon of vinegar. For colored crystals, add a dash of food coloring. Fill up the bowl with porous stones or charcoal. Leave in a safe place without moving for a couple of days. Take it out and notice that crystals have begun to form. As the water continues to evaporate, the bowl will be filled with rock crystals.

find this stone

Directions
While at the beach or walking somewhere with your child, play this game. Ask your child to bring you the smallest stone she can find. Next, ask her to find the smoothest stone. Continue to send her off to locate stones that are round, speckled, wet, colored, white, or too big to carry. This can be a fun vocabulary builder if your child isn't familiar with what the word might mean. Save some of the interesting ones for a rock collection.

water races

Materials
1. Sticks, leaves, twigs

Directions

Find a running stream or watercourse. Decide on a starting line upstream and a finishing line downstream. Put floatable objects (sticks, twigs, leaves, bark) in the water at the starting line and watch to see which ones reach the finishing line first. If the water flows under a bridge or through a tunnel, drop the objects in where the water enters and then run to the other side or end and wait to see which ones arrive first. Your child will soon be able to predict which objects will move faster in the water.

bug safari

Materials
1. Small, clear jars with lids
2. Tweezers or tongs
3. Garden gloves
4. Old spoon

Directions
Plan a walk with your child in the park or woods. Take a backpack with a snack along with the small jars and other materials. As you walk, look for insects (under rocks especially) such as ants, spiders, worms, and snails. Use tweezers, tongs, fingers, or gloves to gently pick them up and place them into the jars. Be on the lookout for insects that might bite or sting and help your child identify the harmless bugs. Take the jars back to your picnic spot and observe the bugs while you eat. Before leaving, return the bugs to their natural habitat.

bird watching

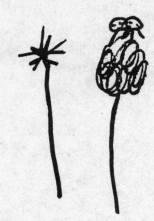

Materials
1. Book about local birds
2. Binoculars

Directions
Check out a library book about the birds in your region. Spend some time looking through the book together and identify some of the birds that you are likely to see in your area. Take the book and a pair of binoculars with you when you go on walks. Watch the birds as they fly or perch. Your child will enjoy looking at the world through binoculars even when he is unable to find a bird to watch. Set out bird food, orange slices, or apples coated with peanut butter on your deck or hang from a tree in your backyard to attract birds to observe.

bark close-up

Materials
1. Magnifying glass
2. Paper
3. Black or brown crayons

Directions
Explore the trees in your neighborhood. Look closely at the bark with a magnifying glass. Close your eyes and feel the texture of the bark with your hands, making sure to touch lightly to prevent splinters. Describe what you feel in words while you are feeling it. Then make a bark rubbing. Take the paper and hold it against the bark. Have your child rub over it with a crayon. Make rubbings of different trees to compare their bark designs. Remember not to peel off the bark of any tree since this would expose the unprotected layers and damage future growth.

create a butterfly garden

Directions

Creating a butterfly garden is easy, even when the only dirt you have available is a planter on your deck! Butterflies are interested in nectar-producing flowers. A few easy-to-find flowers that are known to attract butterflies include zinnias, purple cornflowers, black-eyed Susans, bee balm, butterfly weed, coreopsis, impatiens, ageratum, marigold, and cosmos. Smaller varieties include verbena, alyssum, and impatiens. Your planter will need six hours of sun each day and shelter from the wind. When choosing seeds or nursery plants, make sure to look at the height description of each plant. Plant the taller plants in the back or center of the planter with smaller plants in front or surrounding them. When the flowers begin to bloom, find a stool or small chair to place near the growing plants so children can watch when butterflies arrive. Get a book with pictures of butterflies so you can identify the different varieties when they visit your deck.

bird feeder

Materials
1. Gallon milk carton
2. String, colored yarn, small pieces of fabric
3. Crayons or paint
4. Glue
5. Bird food—seeds, nuts, dried bread, dried fruit

Directions

Cut out large windows from all four sides of the milk carton, leaving two inches, top and bottom. Decorate with crayons, paint, yarn, or fabric. Poke two holes through the top of the carton. Tie the string through each hole. Fill the bottom of the carton with bird food. Put a few pieces of colored yarn in with the food. The birds take the sting and weave it into their nests and sometimes kids can spot a piece of their yarn in a nest they discover. Take the feeder outside and hang it by the strings from a tree. Remember to frequently replace the bird food with a fresh supply.

birdbath spa

Directions

Birds like to frolic in water. Use the clay bottom of a planter or the plastic lid from a garbage can as the base for your birdbath. Decorate the edges with rocks, dried flowers, or paint. Make sure to put a few large rocks in the center so the birds have a place to rest. Set the birdbath on your deck on top of a table, bench, or railing. Wherever you place it, your bird friends will find it! Another variety is the planter birdbath. Take a planter and fill it with dirt. Find the largest plastic bowl or container that will cover one-fourth of the planter. Press the bowl or container into the dirt so the top sticks out about an inch above the dirt. Buy small annual flowers to plant in the dirt around the plastic container. Fill the container with water. Make sure to cut back flowers whenever they block access to the birdbath. Fill birdbaths with water whenever needed.

puddle walk

Directions

Nothing feels better on a warm day than walking through puddles with bare feet. Hold hands for balance. Create big splashes, little splashes, sideways slide splashes, hand splashes, and rock splashes. Jump from one puddle to the next. Observe how the water ripples and moves. See your reflection in the puddle before walking through it. Return the next day to see if the puddle is still there or if it has grown larger or smaller. On colder days wear gumboots or old shoes.

ants on parade

Materials
1. Ants
2. Magnifying glass
3. Crackers

Directions

Have you noticed how children love to watch ants? When you discover a trail, take the magnifying glass and look at the ants close-up. Notice that they have three separate body parts—head, thorax, and abdomen. Count the legs. Place cracker crumbs in the path of the ants and watch the ants carry them away. Ants are social insects and help each other work together. Notice, too, how they meet and greet each other. Follow them until they move out of sight.

centerpiece

Directions
Ask each family member to bring some small object they've found in nature to the dinner table. Together, arrange an attractive centerpiece out of each person's item. Have everyone share the importance of the object they brought, where they found it, and why of all the things they could choose they chose this item to share with the family.

caterpillar to butterfly

Materials
1. Picture books and magazines
2. Photos of the family
3. A picture book showing growth
   stages of humans, such as
   The Family of Man
4. A book about butterflies

Directions
Take the books and look at pictures of all the ages and stages of human growth. Explain how all living things grow and change. Compare photos of family members from childhood until adulthood. Explain that, unlike human babies, who still look like a human when they are grown, caterpillars grow and change, looking very different during each stage as they grow into butterflies. This is called "metamorphosis." Look through the butterfly book and point out the changes from egg to adult.

night hike

Materials
1. Two flashlights

Directions

Plan a night hike with your child. A child's world looks very different at night. It sounds different too. Let your child carry his own flashlight as you carry another. Hold his hand as you explore the garden path or outdoor park. While the adult keeps the path well lit, the child can look around with his own light. Every now and then, stop, turn off the flashlights, and look up at the moon and stars.

rain gauge

Materials
1. Clear glass jar
2. Permanent marker

Directions

On the outside of the jar, have your child mark regular intervals with permanent marker. Use a ruler or some other measure. The point of the marks is to see how much water falls from the sky each time it rains. Place the jar outside where it won't be knocked over. After each rain, check how much rain filled the jar. Empty the jar or keep an ongoing record of how much rain has fallen.

weather diary

Materials
1. Notebook
2. Pencil
3. Crayons

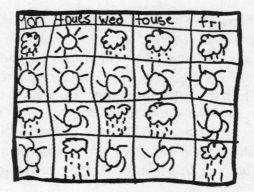

Directions
In a notebook, help your child keep a visual or graphic record of the weather. Perhaps after breakfast each day you could both draw what the weather looks like outside. Use symbols for sunny, rainy, cloudy, and windy, or have your child draw a picture each time. Write in the date and location. Take the weather diary on vacations so that you can document weather changes in different locations. When your child is old enough he can take over the daily entries himself.

winter tracks

Directions
If you are in an area where it snows in the winter or you have large amounts of rainfall so that tracks can be seen in the ground, you can organize a winter tracking expedition. This is best done when the snow is still fresh or the day after a big rain. Look for imprints in the snow or dirt and try to determine which animal might have made them. If necessary, get a book on animal tracks to help you. Follow the tracks and see where they lead. Try making your own tracks while walking, running, and jumping to see how moving tracks look different from standing or walking tracks.

ocean waves

Materials
1. Large plastic soda bottle (not glass)
2. Vegetable oil
3. Blue food coloring
4. Water

Directions
Rinse the bottle and remove labels. Fill the bottle half-full with water, add oil until the bottle is full (including the water). Add a few drops of food coloring. Tightly screw on the bottle cap. Have your child gently rock the bottle back and forth to create waves.

driftwood sea garden

Materials
1. Interesting piece of driftwood
2. Dried seaweed
3. Assorted seashells
4. Glue

Directions
Rinse and dry off driftwood. Set it on a flat surface. Rinse shells and shake the sand out of the seaweed. When all these materials are dry, glue them securely on the driftwood to make a sea garden. Some plant stores sell green plants that look a bit like seaweed that will grow on driftwood without any soil. Use these instead of the dried seaweed if you want to making a living driftwood sea garden.

field and forest sounds

Materials
1. Blanket

Directions
Take your child to an open field, a forest clearing, beach, or park. Spread the blanket and lie down. Listen quietly to nature's sounds. Raise a hand when an interesting sound is heard. Talk about the sound and ask where it came from. Who made it? Was it an animal or a bird or an insect? The wind makes interesting sounds too. Listen to it move through the leaves, the grass, and the trees. Discuss how sounds enhance our experience in nature.

nature book

Materials
1. Notepad
2. Pencil or crayon
3. Glue stick
4. Paper bag

Directions
Take your child on a nature walk with a paper bag and notepad. Stop when you see something the child finds interesting. As your child puts the object in the bag, you can write the location or other details into the notebook. Write down what your child notices about it—color, shape, texture, smell, and surroundings. Continue to collect things and write about them on separate sheets of paper. When you get home, glue the found objects onto the matching written pages and staple the pages together into a nature book.

habitat happenings

Directions

Take a walk through your neighborhood or just go around the block. Notice and discuss all the things that make it a living neighborhood— the people, gardens, plants, lawns, animals, trees, insects, and birds. Explain that all the living things make it a habitat and that town habitats are often different from country habitats. But in order to survive, animals and plants must live together in harmony.

363

my walking stick

Materials
1. Thick, sturdy stick
2. House or furniture paint
3. Paintbrush
4. Sandpaper

Directions

Go on a hike with your child and find a child-size walking stick. Take it home and wash it. Let it dry completely and sand it down with sandpaper until smooth to the touch. Paint the stick with bright colors. Let the paint dry. Now every time you and your child go walking, the painted walking stick can go along. Sticks are great for turning over rocks, poking the earth, and pointing at things.

snail farm

Materials
1. Clear plastic bottle
2. Bean bag or play dough
3. Soil
4. Lettuce or weeds
5. Snails from the garden

Directions
Your snail farm will be contained within the plastic bottle. Cut a small door in the side of the bottle about three inches by two inches, so that when the bottle is on its side the door is at the top. Next, place damp soil in the bottle. Go outside and look for snails in the yard. Look around leafy plants, in the vegetable garden, or at the base of brick walls. Put them in your snail farm and give them fresh food like lettuce and weeds. Seal the door at the top with some clear tape and punch holes in the tape for air vents. Make sure the bottle is sealed. Watch your snails for a few days then let them go.

Snail facts: Snails have 25,000 teeth. The caterpillar slides on its belly, which is called a foot. They leave a slimy trail behind which helps them slide without hurting themselves. That fluid can also be used to seal the shell so the snail can live up to three years without food or water.

Special Thanks

The authors and publishers wish to thank the special group of five- to seven-year-olds from the San Francisco Bay Area who provided all the wonderful illustrations for our book.

About the Authors

Sheila Ellison is the author of nine books; founder of the non-profit organization, Single Moms Connect; creator of an online mothering community www.CompleteMom.com; and a mother of four and stepmother of two. She has appeared on *Oprah!*, and her work has been featured in *O: The Oprah Magazine*, *Parenting*, *Family Circle*, *Ladies Home Journal*, *Glamour, Self*, the *New York Daily News*, the *San Francisco Chronicle*, and the *Oakland Tribune*.

Dr. Judith Gray is internationally known as an author, teacher, leader in dance research, and speaker on future trends in education. A former Executive Director of the Girl's Club of Tucson, Dr. Gray has been an educator at both the high school and university level. A mother of four, she is currently helping to develop state-of-the-art high schools in Washington and is on the Antioch University teaching faculty. Dr. Gray is also the coauthor of *365 Days of Creative Play* and *365 Afterschool Activities* and has also published three books on dance.

Sheila Ellison's
COMPLETE M♥M.COM

Moms are busy people. We need fresh information *right now* about how to have fun with our kids, understand ourselves better, create strong relationships, enjoy our careers, and still have time to make cookies once in a while! Please visit me online at www.CompleteMom.com.

What you will find on this site:
- Parenting articles, advice, and ideas.
- Activities to nurture mom.
- Creative, fun, and interactive activities for every age (including teens).
- Tasty time-tested recipes, party ideas, and games.
- Ideas for building healthy relationships, igniting romance, and having great sex.
- Women's health topics, including exercise, stress release, and nutrition news.
- Chat with other mothers on the extensive message boards.
- Find the words to all your favorite childhood songs.
- Contact Sheila.
- AND MUCH MORE!

Notes

_____

_____

_____

_____

_____

_____

_____

_____

_____

_____

_____

Notes

Notes

Notes

_____

_____

_____

_____

_____

_____

_____

_____

_____

_____

_____

_____

_____

Notes

_____

_____

_____

_____

_____

_____

_____

_____

_____

_____

_____

_____